25 YEARS OF THE

PEACHTREE

Road Race

25 YEARS OF THE
PEACHTREE
Road Race

KAREN ROSEN

LONGSTREET PRESS, INC.
Atlanta, Georgia

To my father, Mel, my coach on and off the track.
To my mother, Joan, a reader not a runner,
who always told me I could do anything I set out to do.
And to Laurie, Chris, Chelsea and Nathaniel.

K. R.

Published by LONGSTREET PRESS, INC.,
a subsidiary of Cox Newspapers,
a division of Cox Enterprises, Inc.
2140 Newmarket Parkway
Suite 118
Marietta, Georgia 30067

Printed in the United States of America

1st printing, 1994

Library of Congress Catalog Number 93-81144

ISBN: 1-56352-127-X

This book was printed by Arcata Graphics Book Group, Kingsport, Tennessee

Jacket and book design by Jill Dible

Photographs Courtesy of the *Atlanta Journal-Constitution*, Atlanta Track Club and Marathon Photo.

Color separations and film produced by Holland Graphics, Inc., Mableton, Georgia.

TABLE OF CONTENTS

Julia Emmons cuts a fine figure finishing second among women in 1972.

I ran my first Peachtree in 1972. I recall only what I wore: polyester shorts, a red sleeveless blouse made of synthetic material much faded by washing, and a paper-thin pair of men's Adidases on my feet. The shoes were four years old and much treasured, as I had not figured out how to get another pair. Size 5 1/2 women's feet were of little interest to running shoe manufacturers. My eyes were shaded by substantial sunglasses, the kind you wear to the beach. The figure I cut had as little dash as my pace per mile.

There were 17 women who ran the race that year, a significant jump from the four who ran in 1971. The men numbered 313. Because they expected only 250 runners, organizers ran out of T-shirts well before I finished. I left, vowing to run fast enough to get a T-shirt next year. But they ran out well before I finished the next year too. Still, I kept coming back.

I was not alone. We all kept coming back, and continue to. In 1993, the limit of 45,000 was reached a scant six days after the opening. In 1994, the field expands to 50,000. What brings us back has changed little since the early seventies. It's something about earning the T-shirt, running down Atlanta's main street, something about the heat, the crowds, the challenges of the hill at mile three. We also come back because we know the race is done for us, we lumpy back-of-the-packers for whom training for the 6.2 miles of Peachtree is a big deal.

To keep the central focus of Peachtree in mind, a few years ago I created a couple of imaginary "Everyrunners," modeled on that polyester-clad self of long ago, whom I nicknamed Dorothy and Frank. They are a bit middle-aged, a tad chubby. Though their running clothes are comfortably styled nylon or supplex, rather than polyester picnic gear, and they wear handsomely constructed Nikes on their feet, they cannot be mistaken for athletes. Finishing Peachtree and earning the T-shirt is their goal. Our task at the Atlanta Track Club is to make sure Dorothy and Frank have a delightful experience this and every Fourth of July they run the race.

We feel sure they will enjoy this book, for they will find themselves throughout, partaking with the talented front runners in the magic of the Peachtree. The race is about the swift and the slow, about Jeff Galloway and Gayle Barron, and Dorothy and Frank in the thousands, joining together to make the race the largest and finest 10K in the world.

Enjoy your portrait.

Julia Emmons
Race Director, 1985–1994

Introduction

The name Peachtree is as intertwined with Atlanta as kudzu. But mention "The Peachtree," and everybody knows what you're talking about.

It's 50,000 people, 100,000 feet and one million toes, give or take a couple, pounding down Peachtree Street on the morning of July 4.

It's Atlanta's version of the Boston Marathon, the running of the bulls in Pamplona and Woodstock, rolled into one.

It's a microcosm of the running boom of the last 25 years and a celebration of body, spirit and community.

It's the world's largest 10K and the biggest participatory sports event east of the Mississippi.

It's runner's high and low blood sugar, sweat mingling with water until you don't know which is yours and which is borrowed.

It's some of the best 10-kilometer runners in the world, and some of the worst; the first batch running for a living, the rest for a T-shirt.

It's seeing that T-shirt all over the world, from the beaches of Israel to the roads of Kenya.

It's 4,000 volunteers who pass out water and T-shirts, organize the race and are everywhere from start to finish.

It's 250,000 spectators who get up early to watch the parade, armed with lawn chairs, garden hoses and encouragement. Some will be inspired to step off the curb next time.

It's a New Year's resolution, a badge of honor, a measure of fitness and a tribute to health and perseverance after illness or injury.

It's a moving social event.

It's open to everyone, with true Southern hospitality, and has literally become a melting pot of people from all over the world. Speed is a prerequisite only in applying.

It's not the heat, of course, that makes it hard. It's the humidity. And the hills.

It's a rite of passage and a right of passage down six lanes of the city's main thoroughfare with no stoplights during this rush hour.

It's a private race, but one in which no one is alone.

It's survival of even the unfittest, everyone pouring out their hearts and soles.

It's the equivalent of a small city hotfooting it 6.2 miles to Piedmont Park, full of every shape, size, ability and work ethic.

It's an offshoot of the same competitive fire that makes people climb a mountain because it's there or sail solo across the ocean. They don't have the time or money to do that, so they run.

It smells like teen spirit, and middle-aged spirit, too.

It's tired legs carried by the crowd and their own determination.

It's the only time some people hear anybody cheer for them.

It's a great common denominator, everybody standing there in their shorts and shirts ready to stampede down the road like a beehive releasing.

It's over by the time most people wake up.

It's crossing the finish line with feelings of euphoria, self-esteem and accomplishment, and a bouquet of roses waiting for the last finisher.

It's a quarter century of growing and

refining, but never redefining.

It's the Peachtree Road Race.

And, said Tim Singleton, the professor who founded the race in 1970, "It's the thing to do. In the early years, it was the thing not to do, like 'You're crazy if you run.' Now, it's, 'You're not running Peachtree? You're crazy.'"

Race director Julia Emmons said the Peachtree's reach is amazing. "If you go into the athletic history of any Atlantan, they have been linked in some way, either themselves or through someone they know, by the Peachtree. Whether they've trained or run or watched, it's in there somewhere." Emmons said the race "somehow touches the soul in a way that is totally unpredictable."

Ruth Rothfarb (right) ran her first Peachtree at age 89.

Peachtree runners can become fanatical about keeping a streak going, refusing to go out of town for the holiday and running through all sorts of sprains and twists and illnesses. Said Ken Bedelle, who hasn't missed a race since 1977, "At some point I have to make the decision to break the string. I don't want to be too compulsive and I've been compulsive enough about it."

It's hard to let go. *The Runner* magazine awarded the race a gold medal and called Atlanta "a true runner's city." *Runner's World* magazine said the Peachtree was its favorite non-marathon, and Atlanta polls have named it the favorite event in the city.

"There's the vision of the last person toeing the line at the start and the first person crossing the finish line," said Emmons, who is also the Atlanta Track Club's executive director. "It's a vision of 6.2 miles of people at any one time."

This human ribbon comprises the largest 10K road race in the world, and third-largest race of any length, behind San Francisco's Bay-to-Breakers (65,000 participants) and the Bloomsday Run in Spokane, Washington (55,000 participants), which are both 12Ks. The Bloomsday Run was patterned after the Peachtree.

There are as many reasons why the Peachtree is successful as there are people running it. Possibly foremost is that it's not a race of 50,000 people, but 50,000 races of one person.

"The desire to do your best and to show your patriotism is what the Peachtree is all about," said wheelchair racer Rod Spence, who ran the race eight times before he was paralyzed in a bicycling accident in 1987. "It gave me the feeling that I could still compete."

"It's the camaraderie," said Gayle Barron, the first female winner when women made up three percent of the field. Now they comprise 30 percent. "It's an event, a

time to socialize, and to be with friends."

"It's like Woodstock," said Alan Ralph. "But once you're in it, it feels like you're in that Merrill Lynch commercial, with that herd of damn stampeding cows. I'm glad it's over, but I wouldn't miss it."

"It's our city's purest happening, proving that people don't have to drink to have a good time," said columnist Ron Hudspeth. (Well, they should drink water.)

"It's a magical, mystical feeling," said three-time winner Craig Virgin. "As the people recognize the lead runner, the volume picks up and swells. It's like the wave at the stadium, and you're riding the crest of the wave." He has also started in the back of the pack with the regular folk. "There's a lot more body odor. I wonder why Right Guard doesn't sponsor it. People are nervous and sweaty."

"I like to watch the second half of the race finish," said Jim Kennedy, chairman and chief executive officer of Cox Enterprises, Inc., which owns the *Atlanta Journal-Constitution*. "It's a sea of humanity, laughing, joking, and a lot of people you would never dream could run a 10K."

"My daughter has not run it before, so I'm escorting her," said Thomas Smith. "It's not a race that a real runner runs. I just do it because it's traditional."

"As long as my knees hold up and as long as my hips hold up, I'm going to keep running," said Kathy Morrow.

"This is my one race a year. I just do it to be part of America," said Roger Shigaki.

"Peachtree is one of my favorites," said four-time winner Grete Waitz. "That's why I like to come back here. I like the people because they're so very nice and supportive. The whole atmosphere to this race is something special."

"Unless somebody has gotten involved in a tractor pull or mud wrestling, I've never seen so many people subject themselves to such torture," said *Atlanta Journal* columnist Furman Bisher. And he's a runner, too, though not of the Peachtree.

And they just keep coming.

"I ran it because I wasn't supposed to be able to do it," said Karen Sliwa, who was battling emphysema.

"Everybody says, 'Why do you get up on the 4th of July and do that miserable thing?'" said Ginger Hamby. "It's like a party. It's fun, like a sweating party. One of my bosses calls it the world's largest wet T-shirt party. It's fun to get in a big bunch of people. Everybody's in a great mood, smiling and laughing and doing something they've prepared for. All the hard work is before."

"You run for an hour and God gives you this natural high, better than any narcotic could possibly be," said Harry Artley. "That's how to celebrate the Fourth."

The serendipitous combination of the holiday and the running boom captured the imagination of the city. From a field of 110 finishers in 1970—actually, quite large at the time—the Peachtree has grown into what the first winner, Jeff Galloway, calls "a national landmark."

"THE CROWD WASN'T AS BIG AS BOSTON, AND YOU DON'T HAVE THE TRADITION HERE AS YET, BUT THAT WILL COME WITH TIME."
— BILL RODGERS, 1976.

"I don't think people think that much (about) what July 4 means," said Singleton, the founding father. "It's a celebration of independence. In a lot of ways, I think running is a celebration of independence, too. Maybe people unconsciously connect those two, and that's been part of the reason for the popularity of the race."

Another factor in the Peachtree mystique has been limiting the field. "If everybody could get in," said Emmons, "it'd lose some of its elusiveness. The fact we sell out in a week and a half gives it an aura it would not otherwise have." And, said Emmons, having to earn the shirt by running the race in 55 minutes—thankfully enforced about as strictly as the 55 mph speed limit—enhances the experience. "For an ordinary citizen, running 6.2 miles is a major accomplishment, although it's within the grasp of nearly everyone if they try."

They run on strong legs and artificial legs, like Scotty Mathis, who represented the Scottish Rite orthotics department.

"The heat and the crowds will slow you down," said course director Bill Royston. "If you're looking for a fast time, I'd go somewhere else. I like to treat this as a party."

Millie Lathan said she gets scared when she sees "so many big men walking up those hills. And the big question is, when you're running, do you wave to the people on the route? That costs seconds."

Barron has run from the front and the back, and she agrees with the back-of-the-packers who claim it's more fun where they are. "There was a lot of elbowing and pushing and shoving when I was running (in front)," she said. "Everybody was out for blood." Her philosophy is it is better to pass than to be passed. "Now I take it with the flow," she said. "It's usually so hot and miserable, it doesn't matter how fast I run it. If I were concerned about my time, I'd get real antsy. People way in the back, all of a sudden they're flying by you 100 mph. Later on you see them half dead at the top of Piedmont Hill. What in the world are they trying to accomplish here?"

In the sea of humanity, there are a few sharks. Claude Crider, one of the original 110 in 1970, recalled trying to go around another runner in a more recent race. "He used his elbow to keep me back," said Crider. "This guy is going to be 23,335th and he's worried about me passing him. You've got to watch those macho guys. I've been passed so many times you get used to it."

"You don't choose hilly Atlanta in the middle of the summer to record a (personal record) time," said 1991 winner Ed Eyestone. "It's more of an endurance race than a speed event."

People talk about the Peachtree in offices, at country clubs and in check-out lines. "You run the Peachtree? So do I." On one level, it's a way of warding off death and illness. People give up smoking and drinking to run, and some get hooked on running instead.

Andrew Young, who was the race's official starter when he was Atlanta's mayor, said the Peachtree "always chokes me up. It really is one of the best symbols of American energy and enthusiasm that I know. The participants are all ages, fami-lies running together . . . it really is one of America's premier sports events."

And he added, "Atlanta built it."

The rest of the world has adopted the race. Ruth Rothfarb of Boston ran her first Peachtree at age 89. Timothy Wyn Harris, a New Zealander whose family owns a sheep farm, learned about the race while reading an article in *National Geographic*. His hometown of Waipukurau held its own version of the race with 600 participants, and pledged money toward the construction of a sports complex for the local state school if he finished the Peachtree. He did.

The race is also a matter of keeping up with the Joneses, or just with the rest of the family. The first time the whole Parker family of Dunwoody ran the race was 1976. Shawn, the youngest of three boys, was eight, and said Nancy Parker, "I was so worried about him that we hired a babysitter to ride a bicycle alongside him." Added Jack Parker, "The babysitter couldn't even keep up with him."

Now the Peachtree doesn't allow eight-year-olds or bicycles.

During the 6.2-mile hike, families support each other, and so do strangers. J. Fred Bailey remembers approaching 14th Street one year and seeing a 12-year-old boy who was struggling. "I got close to him should he need help," said Bailey. "However, before I could speak to him, the boy turned to his father and said, 'Go ahead and finish, Dad. I can't make it.'" His father stopped running, put his hand on his son's shoulder and said, 'No son, we started together and we'll finish together.'" Bailey looked back to see them walking side by side.

Singleton's favorite Peachtree memory dates back 20 years. After giving brief instructions, he got on the starting line. When the gun went off, a young boy to his left tripped. "I just grabbed him by the arm and kind of carried him about 100 feet so

"ARTHUR LYDIARD, NEW ZEALAND'S RUNNING EXPERT CREDITED WITH INITIATING THE JOGGING CRAZE OF THE 1960s. . . PREDICTED THE ENTRY LIST WOULD REACH AS MANY AS 20,000 BEFORE SHOWING A DECLINE."
ATLANTA JOURNAL-CONSTITUTION, 1977.

he could get on his feet," said Singleton. "I was afraid he might have gotten hurt by the masses—or what we considered the masses then. As I set him down, he looked right into my eyes and he was saying thank you, although he didn't say it out loud. And off we went. I never saw him again."

Maria Birdseye was laboring in 1977 when she said, "A guy comes huffing along. He really wasn't a runner but he saw me fading and said, 'C'mon, we can do it.' I thought, what a nice guy that he can care, even though he's not really a runner."

The Peachtree is an introduction to road racing for many people, and for quite a few, it's the only race they run. These athletes-for-a-day come in all sizes, just like the T-shirts. There are more large and extra-large now.

"It leads people to have a lot of social fun," said Singleton. "They say, 'I'm going to get out there and train. I'm going to conquer that physical thing.'

"It's not so much running against other people. It's having covered the distance, hav-

ing met a challenge and conquered it. Plus, it's seeing if you can run down Peachtree Street faster than you can drive it at rush hour, which most people can do."

They also can take part in one of the city's great sporting events. You can't suit up with the Falcons or take batting practice with the Braves, but in the Peachtree, you share the road with world-class athletes. So what if they finish before you start. "They may be down the street, but there's a spiritual bond there," said former race director Bob Varsha.

Many runners don't know who won, however, until they get home. Winning their own race is their only concern.

The Peachtree is actually two races rolled into one: the competitive race and the participatory race. The runner at the back of the pack is treated with as much respect as the world record holder at the front. That's in keeping with Singleton's original vision in 1970. Even as the race attracted famous athletes, the elite field never took on a disproportionate amount of importance.

"We're delighted to have them," said Emmons, "and we're proud to have them, but the emphasis is that each and every one of these people matter a lot to us. And that has led to a loyalty among the back of the pack."

Emmons said for most races, a rule of thumb is 10 percent don't show up, either from sickness or being called out of town. "Except for Peachtree," she said. "People just don't miss it. Only two percent don't show up. Viable statistics don't work in this event. You can't make assumptions or generalizations. In many ways, this is a unique situation."

Emmons designs the race for two mythical people she calls Dorothy and Frank. "They're in time groups five and six, maybe seven. They're a little overweight, in their late 30s, early 40s. A little chubby, not gazelles. They could stand a few less desserts. This is their one event of the year and they're very excited about it."

As the race has matured, it has developed middle-age spread like so many of its runners.

The running boom is reflected in the growth of the Peachtree. In the beginning, said Galloway, Atlanta was one of the few cities in the United States that was ripe for this type of event. Boston was another one, as the Boston Marathon mushroomed in popularity. And San Francisco began the Bay-to-Breakers, which is now known more as a costume race.

"This type of enthusiasm was felt," said Galloway, "and all of a sudden other cities in the U.S. realized, 'Hey, we can do the same thing'. It spread three to five years later throughout the U.S. and the rest of the world, although it took until the late 1980s for it to catch on in some of the European cities."

The success of Frank Shorter in the 1972 and 1976 Olympics, and Shorter's and Bill Rodgers's domination of the Boston

"IT'S NEVER BEEN A MATTER OF BEING THE BIGGEST. WE WERE QUITE READY TO STAY AT 25,000 AND BE THE BEST. WE WOULDN'T HAVE GONE UP TO 50,000 EXCEPT FOR THE BLEATS OF UNHAPPINESS (FROM PEOPLE WHO COULDN'T GET INTO THE RACE). HOW FULL CAN IT GET BEFORE SOMETHING IS LOST? MY SENSE IS WE'RE THERE."
—RACE DIRECTOR JULIA EMMONS, 1993.

Marathon, helped popularize running. Galloway said when he first started running in 1958, there may have been five people above school age in the city of Atlanta who ran, and "maybe there weren't that many." The first running boom in the late 1970s and early '80s was comprised mainly of people in their 20s who tried to run a race every weekend and a marathon a month. "They burned out in '83, '84 and '85," he said. "Large numbers of the running population dropped out in the mid-80s, but at the same time, the new wave of runners started coming in that we're seeing now."

These new runners were in their 30s, 40s and 50s—significantly older than the first group—and they were baby boomers trying to get back in shape.

According to Galloway, "They said, 'Hey, I'm not going to live forever. If I do something about my fitness, my health will be positively affected and I'll have more vitality for the years I have left.'" The stress release and attitude boost gathered from running act as preventive medicine.

The coveted Peachtree shirt is often considered proof of fitness. One tennis player confessed he knew he couldn't wear down another one who was wearing a Peachtree shirt. "When you see that, you know they're not going to get tired," he said.

Galloway and Singleton are alarmed, however, by runners who run only one day a year—July 4 in the Peachtree. "The race

has become such a powerful magnet," stated Galloway, "that a lot of folks who are out of shape use it as their red badge of courage. They say, 'Look, I'm not out of shape. I ran Peachtree.' That's a dangerous perception. One man told me he framed the T-shirt. It was the only time he ran. Fortunately, he survived."

If imitation is the sincerest form of flattery, the Peachtree should blush with pride. Don Kardong, who won Peachtree in 1976, created the Bloomsday Run in its image.

"(Peachtree) has reached this level because there are special things about it or because it was the first of a genre," he said. "It may not have quite the reputation of the Boston Marathon, but almost every runner has heard of the Peachtree. It's something everybody wants to do at least once."

Singleton missed the race in 1976 after he moved to Texas, but at 8:00 a.m., he went out and ran a 10,000-meter loop and cried the whole way. "I felt traumatic and homesick and nostalgic," he said. "The Peachtree was going on and I wasn't there."

Singleton remembers in 1972, at the four-mile mark a car containing a group of all-night partiers drove by, and someone called out, "Why are you running?" Before Singleton could answer, a young boy beside him yelled back, "I'm running for myself."

As the Peachtree Road Race enters its second quarter-century, officials are still putting on the race for that boy and the other 49,999. "I think it succeeds because it's so unselfish," said Bob Brennan, a former ATC president and the finish-line announcer. "There was no self-aggrandizement among the organizers. Nobody got a lot of money out of it. It had that feel about it: amateurism at its best, put on in a very professional way.

"Nobody set out to say, 'Let's get a record number here'. Take a look at the people involved. They were just people who wanted to do a good job of putting on an event in which people could par-

ticipate and have a good time."

Emmons said she and her staff will never make changes to the Peachtree without a great deal of thought. "Whatever it is that makes it magical, we can't tinker with," she said. "It's like an orchid, very fragile. A little bit of mishandling, a little greed or overcommercialization would ruin it." Emmons believes that in life, the most successful human beings are very comfortable with who they are and are not trying to be like anybody else. She believes the same philosophy applies to road races. "We have not looked to Bay-to-Breakers and wanted to have centipedes," she said. "We haven't looked at the New York Marathon, and the glitz and glamour and media attention. The Peachtree has steadfastly been a family-oriented, back-of-the-pack event. It is supremely well-organized because of the heat. We can't take chances with sloppiness.

"In the early days we were learning by doing. We had nowhere to look to learn. We were out front."

And they still are.

PEACHTREES PAST

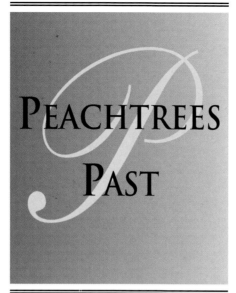

It's fitting that the Peachtree Road Race was born on the Fourth of July. It began as a declaration of independence from a race which not only was considered elitist, but was also way out of town.

Tim Singleton, who calls himself "sort of the thinker-up of the idea," had twice driven a carload to Fort Benning for a five-mile July 4 race. "Their heart was in the right place, but they only seemed interested in the first three places and nobody else after that," said Singleton, then the dean of men at Georgia State and cross country coach. "They didn't give times or anything."

To Singleton, all runners are created equal. On the way home in 1969, carrying Bruce LaBudde's first-place trophy—so big they had to fold the backseat down in the station wagon and so expensive it would have paid for 100 smaller prizes—Singleton and his runners talked about staging their own race. "We were always talking about crazy weird races to run."

Jeff Galloway, who won the first Peachtree and became a great patron of the race, insists that "they were under the influence of a couple of Coca-Colas or something. Tim took this on as a mission."

And Singleton kept in mind what would become the Peachtree philosophy of treating the last-place finisher with as much

consideration as the first.

Singleton thought about running the race at Stone Mountain, but backed off after trying it himself—a good thing since the granite rock would never have been big enough to hold the current field. He decided to start the race in Buckhead, and picked the 10K distance, rather than the more popular five, six, eight or 10-milers, because the Olympics were coming up in 1972, and he wanted people to be able to compare the Peachtree to the Olympic 10K. "It was interesting to hear people say, 'Now, is 10,000 meters a marathon?'"

The race met with some resistance. Tom Aderhold, a member of the Atlanta Track Club, told Singleton, "No way people could be induced to run in the heat on the Fourth."

But Singleton kept plugging along. He got a parade permit, and lined up four motorcycle policemen, one for the lead and three to zip along the route. Unfortunately, they didn't come on duty until 9:30 a.m., so the race had to start as the day warmed up. However, the usual Atlanta Track Club races began at 5:00 p.m., and those were really hot.

Singleton first measured the course with his car's odometer, then a week before the race he drove a van with a measuring wheel while Tom Raynor, one of his Georgia State cross country runners, ran a mile

Bob Varsha became the Peachtree's first full-time director in 1979. Varsha, an attorney, took the job thinking he'd have enough time to train for the 1980 U.S. Marathon Trials. Sorry, Bob.

at a time. They would then stop and spray paint the pavement. On race day, Singleton marked the course with cooking flour.

Singleton had an inkling he was on to something big, and decided to seek sponsorship from a local television station to pay for prizes. He got in to see the WSB general manager mainly because he was a former neighbor. He said for $500, WSB could have exclusive TV rights. "He looked at me like I was crazy," said Singleton. "He almost threw me out of his office."

Twelve years later WTBS aired the race live all over the world.

Singleton was still looking for a sponsor when an executive from the Carling Brewery—now closed—asked the six-year-old Atlanta Track Club to help put on a family field day with such events as races and a beer keg toss. Singleton said the ATC would help in return for sponsoring the

race, and "that's how it got to be the Carling Peachtree Road Race."

The race began at the Sears building at East Paces Ferry and Peachtree, later a casualty of time and space.

Gayle Barron was one of three women in the race. She had never run more than two-and-a-half miles before, and only on the track, never the roads.

"I didn't do it to be different," she said. "I did it because I loved to run, and nobody else was running much. There was such camaraderie. There were 110 runners who immediately began to be friendly and know each other."

As soon as stragglers passed a side-street, the barricade would be removed and everything would be back to normal.

Were there spectators? "Pfffttt," said Barron. "No. Except people staring at us. To everybody else we were weirdos. Who's that idiot running down the street? It was not really the thing to do."

She joked about the trophy she received, "mainly because there were no breasts on the woman." Of course not. It was a man.

Had the race been scheduled for July 3 or 5, maybe the same 110 would have been there. Maybe not.

"I'm not the greatest of prophets," said Galloway, "because never in my wildest dreams did I think we'd ever have 25,000 runners. But I knew we had something special."

The Peachtree would eventually become Atlanta's short answer to the Boston Marathon. Some people felt like they had run a marathon due to the three H's: hills, heat and humidity.

The *Atlanta Journal-Constitution* covered the inaugural race more for the freakish nature of the event than as a serious sports story.

But, said Singleton, "People seemed to be more excited than at other races. I just had the feeling we'd hit upon a good thing here. No telling where this might go."

Because running was still considered "to be a really weird thing," Singleton had difficulty drumming up coverage the next year. He hand-delivered the results to a newspaper writer, and he recalled, "As I walked out, I turned and watched him put them in the circular file (trash can). That was a little discouraging."

But people had a good time and word got out. Whole families took part, like the Bolts of Huntsville, Alabama and the Gamels of East Point. They vied for some of the various awards that gave the Peachtree its neighborly appeal: largest family, father-son, youngest finisher, top brothers, fastest finisher over 200 pounds, etc.

The Bolts often won the Bolt award which actually had a bolt on it. "You could do things like that," said Maria Birdseye. "It was so small. Everybody knew everybody. It was nice."

But John Oeltmann, 60, of Fort Walton Beach, complained in 1972, "Every time I run in anything, I win the old man's trophy."

Children often beat adults. Karen Gamel, the second female finisher in 1974, was 10 years old. She said her friends were too lazy to run, and she enjoyed beating men and boys.

The race received a bigger write-up in the *New York Times* than the local papers. The *Times* wrote that it was "one of the nation's newer Fourth of July observances," and was "perhaps less daring than General Sherman's march down Peachtree, but it was at least as courageous as Mao Tse Tung's swimming the Yangtze."

As part of the modest post-race celebration at the Trust Company Plaza, a refreshment table manned by members of the TKE fraternity at Georgia State provided cokes to competitors free—"You will be able to tell who they are," said the

instructions—and to everybody else for 25 cents.

The official results booklet showed a barefoot runner with bandaged feet standing on the pavement next to his shoes and socks.

Unlike today, there was no limit to the number of entrants, but they had to meet strict qualifications. Runners had to prove their fitness by meeting at least one of these criteria:

* Run at least 100 miles during June of 1972
* Compete in a sanctioned race of at least six miles, 90 days before July 4, 1972, and give the name of the race and the time
* Submit a doctor's certification of fitness
* Be a runner of "known" ability and fitness

The promotional flyer for the race asked, "Have you ever wondered if you could run from Buckhead to Downtown Atlanta faster than you could drive that distance? Have you ever had a secret desire to run down Peachtree Street?"

The running community in the Southeast was a close-knit group, and Singleton could count on publicity in club newsletters from Alabama, Florida and South Carolina. In 1972, he even reserved several motel rooms for the newsletter editors, who then "went back and wrote great things about the Peachtree Road Race. That contributed to a significant increase in people running."

In 1974, the Carling Brewery decided to rename the race for its premium beer, and the Tuborg Peachtree Road Race was on tap. Bill Neace set up a masters division within the ATC—"All right you ol' guys! Unite!"

The entire budget was $3,375: $2,875 from Carling and $500 from entry fees.

Before wheeled vehicles and children under 10 were banned, both pulled their share of attention.

The T-shirts cost $1,233.27 (over the budgeted $900), post-race refreshments $104.52, safety pins $10.03, advertising and promotional expense $17.03, and elite athlete Barry Brown's expenses amounted to $50.

The race still had some growing pains. Alan Salzman wrote Singleton that he was under the impression policemen would stop cross traffic. "I came close to being run down at North Avenue as a policeman sat on his motorcycle smoking his cigar and watching as three cars moved through the intersection," Salzman said. He also politely inquired of the possibility of having a "genuine, sincere timer at each mile point, rather than the nuts and bystanders who call out erroneous clockings."

Competitors, for their part, had a few rules to follow. The Competitor Information Sheet required that runners wear shirts, an AAU rule, pin their number on the front of their shirt, pin their ID tag on the back of the right shoulder and run in the extreme right traffic lane. At the finish, the ID tag would be marked with the place and torn off for determination of final results—as long as the runner finished in 65 minutes or less.

In 1975, a new feature the night before the race was a clinic featuring top runners. These clinics at Jeff Galloway's store, Phidippides, would discuss topics such as "Training and Nutrition," "Foot Care and Blisters" and "How to Stay Cool on July 4."

The race grew from 110 to just over 1,000 in the first six years. As each runner crossed the finish line, he'd get a card with his name and time on it—and depending on whether he earned a T-shirt—the shirt, a can of Gatorade, 15 cents for the bus ride back to Buckhead and an ATC meet schedule. Even then, there were a few grousers. Some of the late finishers complained they didn't get a can, and empty Gatorade cans kicked on the sidewalk disturbed local residents.

The race hit a sponsorship crisis when the Carling Brewery, which was not doing well financially, tried to back out two months before the 1975 race. Singleton wouldn't allow it, but Carling did yank its slogan at the last minute, ruining Singleton's plans for a classy T-shirt. Celebrity pitchmen would tout the beer by saying, "I'm so-and-so, and I've got class." Singleton wanted the shirts to say, "I've got class," but Carling called the day before the deadline and told him the slogan had been changed to "Tuborg Beer is a very good beer." Said Singleton, "No wonder they went out of business."

This was also Singleton's last year as race director. He got his doctorate and moved to Houston, leaving the race in the hands of Bill Neace and Billy Daniel.

Then the Peachtree decided to go bigtime. Carling pulled out for good, and the new directors approached Jim Kennedy at the *Atlanta Journal-Constitution*, then the assistant to the president of Cox Enterprises, Inc., and now chairman and chief executive officer, about obtaining sponsorship. "I made a few calls, and executives would look at me like, 'What the hell are you talking about?' I thought, 'Why doesn't the newspaper sponsor it?'" said Kennedy. "It doesn't cost much and it's a neat little thing."

Kennedy went to Jack Tarver, then the publisher and a gruff guy, and inquired about sponsoring the race. "I don't like car races," growled Tarver. No, corrected Kennedy, "This is a running race down Peachtree. It'll be a good thing for the city. Running is coming on."

Tarver asked if he had the money in the budget. Kennedy fudged a bit, and found it. With his encouragement, the race increased its visibility within the community as the paper provided not only money, but publicity and promotion. The day before the 1976 race, a full page ad

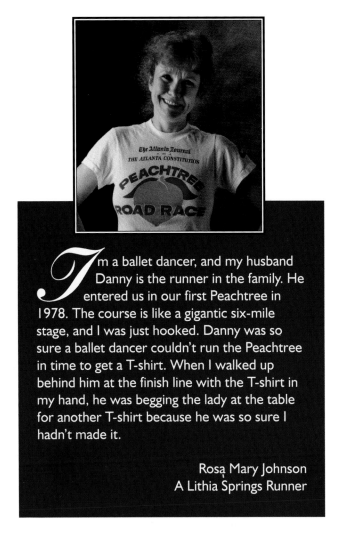

I'm a ballet dancer, and my husband Danny is the runner in the family. He entered us in our first Peachtree in 1978. The course is like a gigantic six-mile stage, and I was just hooked. Danny was so sure a ballet dancer couldn't run the Peachtree in time to get a T-shirt. When I walked up behind him at the finish line with the T-shirt in my hand, he was begging the lady at the table for another T-shirt because he was so sure I hadn't made it.

Rosa Mary Johnson
A Lithia Springs Runner

listed all of the early entries.

Kennedy said the newspaper decided to sponsor the race because it stressed physical fitness, and because "the average person who runs two miles a day can run and feel he's accomplished something. What we want to do is build it into something that is big *and* good."

"The road race could have died at least for a few years if the newspapers hadn't picked it up in the beginning," admitted Galloway. "The papers helped make it an event."

The idea was to stage a race that would be world-class and invite some of the best runners in the world. Galloway was the go-between because he was friendly with the top runners, such as 1976 champion Don Kardong and runner-up Bill Rodgers. "At first, they came as a favor to me," he said. "The second year, I didn't have to convince them at all." Olympic champions Frank Shorter and Lasse Viren of Finland joined the 1977 field.

The second new phase was promoting the event as a race for the public at large, a vehicle for getting people off the couch and on the roads, increasing the general fitness of the population.

In 1977, Galloway also invited Kenny Moore, a 1968 Olympic marathoner and writer for *Sports Illustrated*. Moore wrote a story that praised the international field while conveying the spirit and excitement of the common folk.

"As a result, the people came; sort of like the *Field of Dreams*," said Galloway. "There was such publicity that Peachtree was established as *the* road race in the world."

An article in *Runner's World* spelled Peach Tree in two words, and most who wrote to Singleton playfully spelled it the same way, also misspelling Singleton's name the same way as the magazine. Nevertheless, the race was famous, and also made the *World Book Encyclopedia Year Book*.

The draw of the high-caliber field and increased attention to physical fitness caused the 1976 race to be overrun by entrants. Organizers expected 1,500 and got 2,350. In the parking lot at Sears, they were tearing up shopping bags to make numbers. On the other end, there were no times after No. 399 because of the backup at the finish chute which made the times erroneous.

"In those days, we were standing at the finish line with a stopwatch, which was about as useful as Davy Crockett's muzzleloader at the Alamo," said Bob Varsha, a two-time race director. Organizers apol-

ogized for the inconvenience. "We'll be ready for all of you next year and more."

That number was tripled in 1977, with 6,500 runners. Of that number, 4,110 pre-registered, and the other 2,400 registered late. Late registration was eliminated altogether in 1979 because of logistics and, said Varsha, to cut down on "the people who might make a last-second decision to run in the race when they're not fit."

Because there was no ATC office, Galloway donated the back room at his Phidippides store from 1976–78 for track club business. "It was an exciting time," said Galloway. "We had world-class athletes flowing through, as well as average people trying to figure out how to train for this thing."

Neace applied up-to-date business skills to race management, but as the Peachtree grew more successful, some factions engaged in a bit of a tug of war over this lucrative commodity. Shoe giant Nike, one of the sponsors, wasn't comfortable with the idea of running a race out of a shoe store, and track club members also feared the race was becoming too associated with a commercial entity, Phidippides.

Within the track club, there were disagreements about how to handle the $50,000-$60,000 in entry fees (whether to use the money to bring in top athletes), and how to capitalize on the running boom. The race for many years threatened to become the tail that wagged the dog of the track club, and some members thought there was too much emphasis on the race.

The newspaper stayed out of the arguments and quietly trademarked the race as the *Atlanta Journal-Constitution* Peachtree Road Race. The track club found out and was outraged, and there arose the possibility of competing Peachtrees. The matter was settled, however, and said Varsha, "Through all of this, there was such an abiding affection for the race that it always seemed to win out."

The Peachtree goes big-time in 1976, with Jeff Galloway (left) inviting fellow Olympians Bill Rodgers and Don Kardong to take part in his little Atlanta race. Kardong won the race, with Rodgers second.

Varsha became the first full-time director, and set up shop in 1979 in an old building on Peachtree with a couple of secretaries. He then turned over the reins the next year to Royce Hodge, who bought the little house on East Shadowlawn, near the one-mile mark, which is still race headquarters.

In 1979, there were an estimated 22,000 finishers and 3,000-4,000 unregistered runners, causing Hodge and the race committee to assert control by limiting the number of entries in 1980. The race would close when entries reached 25,000 or on May 23, whichever came first. It was simultaneous.

"The years from 1979–84 were a magical time," said Craig Virgin, who won the Peachtree from 1979–81. "Road racing was a phenomenon. Fields were doubling each year. Fitness and running were almost synonymous. The definition of fitness was, 'Can you go out and run?' and the 10K was the epitome."

As the sport matured, the fringe people dropped out, said Virgin, but there was

Grete Waitz of Norway won four Peachtrees.

still growth. "Race administration was a newfound industry, struggling to cope with the demands and pressure put upon it."

After the 1981 race, the newspaper decided to withdraw as the title sponsor, and did not return until 1985. New sponsors came and went, and in 1984, the ATC doubled the entry fee from $5 to $10. One runner sent in his entry blank completely filled out, then with a magic marker he wrote, "Hell no, I won't pay $10 for 10K." He was in the minority, however, as there were a record number of entries.

"This is something that was very painful for the track club to do," said race director Roy Benson. "We certainly agonized over it and tried to find ways to get around it, but there was no way. The track club board of directors had to be sure the race paid for itself."

More arguments arose over the awarding of prize money and appearance fees. The Peachtree paid expenses, but opposed appearance fees. "That's one of the things we put our foot down on," said Varsha. "Running the Peachtree was a privilege and not a right."

When the Peachtree also decided not to pay prize money from 1978–81, its reputation fell. There were complaints the race wasn't attracting enough big names, and the Bay-to-Breakers had outpaced its growth. The Peachtree wasn't the biggest race any more.

Virgin bemoaned the lack of prize money, although he kept coming back. "I feel in some ways that the management operates as if Peachtree is Peachtree, and the guys should come just because of that," he said. "The world doesn't work that way anymore."

The establishment of trust funds led to the appearance of prize money in 1982—$5,000 each to Jon Sinclair and Anne Audain—and that helped the race regain its stature. However, Virgin called the purse paltry compared to the overall quality of the event.

The Peachtree purse now is $50,000, divided equally among male and female

runners and with $5,000 still going to the winners. The race is an event on the Association of Road Racing Athletes Circuit, which offers a combined $1 million in purses and end-of-season bonuses.

A STUDY BY THE CENTERS FOR DISEASE CONTROL'S CARL CASPERSEN SAID IF YOU RUN 15 MILES A WEEK, YOU CAN EXPECT TO BE HIT BY A THROWN OBJECT ONCE EVERY 12 YEARS, BITTEN BY A DOG ONCE EVERY 26 YEARS, HIT BY A CAR ONCE EVERY 135 YEARS AND RUN OVER BY A BIKE ONCE EVERY 539 YEARS.

"We try to do essentially what the PGA and the Association of Tennis Professionals do, certainly with smaller amounts of money," said Kardong, president of the ARRA. "There's probably 200-300 runners that look at this group of events seriously. These are people who make their living running, or supplement their income."

There was still the separate question of appearance fees. In 1982, Australian marathoner Rob de Castella was invited to run, but talks broke down when he demanded an appearance fee, which violated the membership rules of the ARRA.

Also in 1982, the race hit a major roadblock—the opposition of the churches along the races' route to running on Sunday. After much negotiation and thundering from the pulpits, the race time was moved back half an hour to 7:30 a.m.

Marathon Foto snapped into action in 1983, taking pictures of every runner from a makeshift bridge above 14th street. They had 3,000 extra people to photograph thanks to a computer error.

In 1984, two sacks of runners packets were found at the post office, causing 2,000 runners and the ATC to scramble.

The 1985 race brought a showdown between the ATC and The Athletics Congress, track and field's national governing body, over the entry of South African Ashley Johnson. The ATC supported Johnson. However, on the eve of the race, Johnson withdrew from the race voluntarily so he would not "contaminate" the other runners. He had competed the year before with no problem. Craig Virgin said he had no opposition to Johnson but now fears the Peachtree has gone "overboard" and "gotten out of balance in terms of percentage of foreign athletes."

Between Sinclair's victory in 1982 and Ed Eyestone's in 1991, the Peachtree was won eight years by foreign athletes— Kenya (four times), Tanzania, Ireland, Belgium and Mexico. Kenya swept the top three places three times (1985, 1992 and 1993). The top American finisher was 10th in 1993 and there were only three American-born male racers in the Top 23. In the women's field, the Top 10 had only three Americans.

"In my day, we had to compete almost exclusively against Americans," said Kardong. "But since prize money came in, the U.S. has become the place to be for top runners from all over the world."

Furthermore, he stated, "We certainly don't have as many great American runners as we did during the glory years of the '70s and '80s. Other countries are producing a greater number of superior talents."

Explained Kenyan Sam Ngatia, "We grow up with runners as heroes. The children in America grow up with football and basketball players as idols. In America, kids get up and ride their bikes to the corner or to school. In Africa, they run."

Virgin believes the crowd misses cheering an American winner. "They didn't appreciate the fact that I was an American

Tony Pettit limbers up in the parking lot at Lenox in 1980 with an available car.

until later," he said. "So many foreign athletes didn't speak English and people had a hard time relating to them. I could give good interviews; people got to know me as a person."

For its part, the women's field has had an inordinate amount of New Zealanders among the top five finishers, but also plenty of American winners—especially when Norway's Grete Waitz skipped the race. However, there have been complaints about an overall lack of depth. In 1987, third-place finisher Marty Cooksey said the women's field was not as competitive as the men's. "I don't want to be a traitor to my own gender, but when I look at how many top men are vying for the top places and then you look at the women, it's obvious there's just not as much depth. There's a big, intimidating gap between the top women and the rest."

Most Peachtree runners, however, didn't care who was running in the front of the pack as long as they were behind them. The race's increase in numbers from

25,000 to 40,000 to 45,000 and now 50,000 are a by-product of one of the basest human emotions: "Anger," said Emmons.

The 1989 Peachtree Road Race reached its 25,000-runner limit just nine days after applications were accepted. About 15,000 people were shut out. "People were absolutely furious," said Emmons. And desperate.

Back in 1970, no one could have imagined how popular or huge the race would become. The Peachtree enables the ATC, which has 10,000 members, to fund the rest of its events, including about 30 other races.

"People are always asking me about the first Peachtree," said Singleton. "Nobody ever asks me about the first and only Lake-Winfield-State-Park-to-Vogel-State-Park-and-Back-Again race.

"I think I get too much praise and credit," he admits. "It's the people who came and ran in it those early years. If they hadn't come, we wouldn't have had the race. It doesn't seem to me such a creative thing, but I guess it had to start somewhere. I'm glad it did."

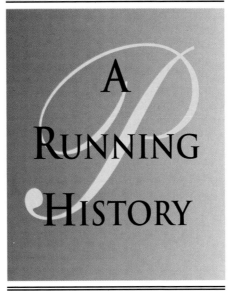

A RUNNING HISTORY

1971

Bill Herren of Pensacola, Florida, was first among 198 finishers ages 7 to 65. He beat Scott Eden with a winning time of 30:58. There were six father-son teams and two husband-wife teams, including Gayle and Ben Barron. In a repeat of the year before, Gayle nipped Ben at the tape, both sharing a time of 45:17. Carling gave out Gatorade instead of its own brew.

1972

With a field of 322, the Peachtree became the largest race in the Southeast.

Scott Eden, an Atlanta resident and Duke student who had set a national age group record for six miles at age 17, won with a time of 31:10. He broke away from Kenneth Layne at the three-mile mark and won by almost a minute. The times were slower than before because the course had been remeasured and was found to have been short. After the race, Eden hopped a plane to fly out west and run against the Russians.

Jeff Galloway and Gayle Barron both skipped the race, Galloway to qualify for the Olympic team, and Barron to go to Florida for vacation.

Gillian Valk was the women's winner. After watching the race in 1971, she decided to run in 1972, and her winning time was 47:42. "I don't think there was a soul watching except the odd spouse who was daft enough to get up that early," said Valk. "At the time, I really didn't think it was that special. It was just the race for the month of July."

The Bolts of Huntsville, Alabama, won the family award with six runners.

1973

Bill Blewett of New Boston, Texas, used his 4:02-mile speed to outkick Scott Eden by four seconds with a time of 31:22. Blewett had flown to Atlanta to visit an old Army buddy, who met him at the airport with the news that he had entered him in the race. Nevermind that Blewett couldn't stand running in the heat. Of the 548 starters, 525 finished in the time limit of 65 minutes. For the first time, there was a crowd of several hundred spectators.

Gayle Barron resumed her winning ways with a time of 40:37. Husband Ben, naturally, finished a step behind with the same time. Barron was named most improved, having bettered her own record by 4:20. Gillian Valk, the 1972 winner, was second among the women.

Thomas Osano, a late entrant, was first to the finish line in 1993.

Craig Virgin wins the first of three Peachtrees in 1979 with a pose that Adidas used in a full-page advertisement with the slogan "We've got a feeling for winning."

There were 225 early entries, and about 300 more the morning of the race. The last recorded time was 64:15 for No. 505, Paul Newmark, who won the award for being the biggest runner. The temperature had climbed to 87 degrees before the 65-minute limit was up, and seven people were taken to Grady Hospital.

Nick Costes, a 1956 Olympian, won the 40-49 division.

One of the last runners was Larry Woods, a speech writer for Vice Mayor Maynard Jackson. "I ran to protest

Nixon," Woods said. A man nearby was asked what he had run to protest and he said, "Nothing. I ran in favor of sex."

Two middle-aged runners stood in the park after the race drinking beer, and one asked the other, "Did you get chills?" "No," he answered, "I got hallucinations."

1974

This was "The Year it Rained" and "The Year They Ran the Wrong Way." Neither has happened since.

There had been thunderstorms earlier in the morning, and the race was run in a soft drizzle.

Scott Eden and Olympic steeplechaser Barry Brown were running 1-2 when they got to the turnoff at West Peachtree. "I couldn't remember which way to go," said Eden. "A policeman directed us down Peachtree. I was so used to following that I followed Barry. When they realized we were off course, they took us back by making a right turn and going over two blocks. By then we were in 12th and 13th, and finished fifth and seventh."

Wayne Roach of the Atlanta Track Club, who had been in third place, knew the course and also saw the arrow on the pavement put there by race director Tim Singleton with cooking flour. He was the winner among the 765 finishers with a time of 30:47 and was the last Atlanta resident to win the overall title.

The prize for the first five finishers was a portable black and white television set worth about $80. Singleton felt bad for Eden, who probably would have gotten a TV set if he hadn't gone the wrong way. So he got one for him, too. The sixth-place finisher, Greg Camp, Roach's coach, was left out. Ironically, he was the buddy 1973 champion Bill Blewett had come to visit the year before.

average Atlanta citizen could remember."

His biggest sponsor, Adidas, wanted him to run Peachtree, so Virgin complied. With a course record time of 28:30.5 on a difficult course, he leaped through the tape with his arms uplifted and fingers in a "V" for victory sign. That photo became a famous Adidas ad with the caption, "We've got a feeling for winning."

For three years, Virgin had that feeling. When he found out that Frank Shorter had pulled out of the 1979 race, he boldly predicted he would win in a Joe Namath-like move. Asked if Shorter's withdrawal made a difference, Virgin said, "Frank who?" and smiled.

Shorter's spokesman said he withdrew to concentrate on the Pan American Games in Puerto Rico, but it was whispered that Shorter was upset with Peachtree officials for using his name in connection with the race before he had given his absolute assurance he would run.

Virgin dined on frog legs the night before the race as part of a six-course meal and said, "I'm willing to try anything. The frog legs helped me get up that hill."

Roche had a four-yard lead at Peachtree Hills, but by the top of Cardiac Hill, Virgin was in command.

The women's winner was an unknown. Heather Carmichael, an 18-year-old New Zealander headed for Penn State, became the youngest Peachtree winner of either sex. She was touring with her coach on the road racing circuit and was primarily a 1,500-meter runner who had run only one other 10K in her life. She took the lead 500 meters from the finish when Margaret Groos passed out, and finished in a time of 33:38.67.

Carmichael said she hadn't seen the course before, but had seen a map, "so I knew where the hills were."

Jeff Galloway, the first Peachtree winner, was presented a trophy for "running the extra mile" down the years to make

the race a success.

One expected entrant was a no-show. Atlanta mayor Maynard Jackson missed the race, blaming bad ribs from the night before. He backed it up by missing the July 4 parade, too.

1980

Craig Virgin, the brash defending champion, predicted he would win again, and he was right.

About three-fourths of the way up Cardiac Hill, he approached a fire hydrant spray a step behind Kenyan Sosten Bitok. By the other side of the spray, Virgin was ahead. He said his winning time of 28:39.04 "soothed the pain of the U.S. Olympic boycott."

"It was hot as blazes," said Virgin. One of his tactics was to focus on the press truck and sometimes wink at the reporters. "I would try to read their lips

Gayle Barron receives one of her five first-place women's awards from race founder Tim Singleton. There was a small brass-plated man on her first trophy.

Courtesy of Gayle Barron

and figure out what they were saying so I could disassociate from my pain and fatigue," he said. Virgin would also race the press truck, forcing it to speed up.

Patti Lyons-Catalano paced herself to win in a record time of 32:48.5. Her time would have beaten everybody but Jeff Galloway in the first Peachtree, and that course was found to be short. Lyons-Catalano won by nearly two minutes over Carol Urish. The previous year, she had paid the price with pains in her stomach. "This time I started out conservatively and saved up for the second half of the course—which is the worst," she said. Lyons- Catalano came in two spots ahead

of her husband-coach, Joe. "I'm happy when she beats me," he said.

Jacqueline Gareau, who won the 1980 Boston Marathon once Rosie Ruiz was disqualified, was in second place when she collapsed inside Piedmont Park with 500 meters to go.

The Peachtree had its first fatality when runner Curtis McMillan went into a coma and died seven months later.

1981

Live, on national television, Craig Virgin won his final—and most meaningful— Peachtree in a thrilling duel with New Zealand's Rod Dixon. He won by 60 yards in an American record time of 28:03.4, while an astounding 46 men followed him under 30 minutes.

Virgin took the lead at four miles. "I looked around at the crest of the hill at Colony Square (the course then went up 14th Street) and was shocked to see Dixon just five yards back," he said. "But I had the lead going into Piedmont Park and I knew that park." He used the turns to his advantage, accelerating when he was out of Dixon's sight. "I gave everything I had that day," said Virgin. "I was white and shaking afterward. With Dixon on my tail, see, there was no way I could relax. I've never had anyone stay with me so long. Let me tell you, I was hoofing it. I was scared."

"Scared?" said Dixon. "Quite rightly so, he should have been scared." Dixon said he thought the Colony Square Hill would be tougher, and when it wasn't, "That's when I knew I gave the race to Craig."

Another New Zealander, Allison Roe, was the women's champion. Two other New Zealanders, Anne Audain and Glenys Quick placed in the top five. Roe said she had heard bad reports about

Lynn Jennings breaks the tape.

Peachtree, "and I really didn't want to come. I wasn't looking forward to it."

Her mood didn't improve when she arrived. She said she didn't sleep well the night before because someone nearby was having a party. She had a small Coke for breakfast and took an hour to get to the start.

There, she assumed a more positive frame of mind. "A 17-year-old boy asked if he could run along with me," she said. "I said, 'Sure, I'd like the company.' He stayed right with me until the end."

Someone who didn't was Mary Decker, who tripped on one of those reflectors between traffic lanes and fell to the pavement. Lee Fidler saw her, and he said, "Perhaps I hesitated for a second, but the next thing I knew, I was sliding down Peachtree beside her. It was truly a terrifying experience. Mary was screaming, and we were surrounded by feet, feet, feet. My life flashed before my eyes. 'This is it,' I thought'. I'll be trampled to death at Peachtree. That's a fitting way for a runner to die.'" Fidler scrambled to his knees, shielding his face from all the knees and elbows, and a passing runner grabbed his arm and pulled him up. He found out later it was Jeff Parker, a member of one of the Peachtree's first families.

Decker also got up, and finished the race, but it was such an unpleasant experience she never returned.

1982

Jon Sinclair, wearing tacky flowered Hawaiian print trunks, outkicked Michael Musyoki and Adrian Leek in the park for the win. His time of 28:17 was a personal best by 20 seconds. Sinclair was the last American to win until 1991.

"I just got tired," said Musyoki, world record holder for a 10K on the roads

with a time of 27:47. "I could not move any more."

"I ran out of gas," said Leek.

"I just kept holding on," said Sinclair.

Craig Virgin, who was recovering from a kidney infection, was sixth.

Anne Audain, continued the New Zealand streak in the women's race with a time of 32:35.3. She said she was on her way to Disney World. She had been second to Roe in 1981; this time she said she never saw another woman in the fast-paced race.

1983

In a race of thrills and spills, Michael Musyoki won the closest Peachtree ever, edging fellow Kenyan Joseph Nzau by a shoelace, 28:21.6 to 28:21.8.

The start was just as exciting, with Grete Waitz, the women's eventual winner, falling and getting pulled to her feet by her brother. Waitz had skinned her thigh badly, but still won in a course record time of 32:00, which lasted until 1992. Dorthe Rasmussen was second in 33:13.

Waitz, the only living Norwegian besides the King to have a statue in her honor, had been afraid she would fall at the start. Waitz didn't fall; she was pushed.

"I ran five meters, then I was on the ground," she said. "Someone knocked me over, and 30 people ran over me. It went through my mind, 'That was the race.' I almost stopped. I about started to cry. I ran to win it." And she did. Her brother, Jan Anderson yanked her up and put her on her feet.

Although Waitz had lost sight of the other female runners, she ran down Rasmussen at two kilometers, then made her move on the hills. As the humidity irritated her wounds, Waitz said, "I tried not to think about it, but it was hard when it started to burn. I don't consider what I would have done if I hadn't fallen."

Wrapped in gauze as she limped away from the first-aid area, someone commented that Waitz needed a fife and drum and would be the perfect Independence Day champion.

As temperatures hovered around 80 degrees, Musyoki, runner-up the year before, could never shake Nzau. "I felt I was opening up," he said, "but he was very strong. When I opened up, he came back. Anything can happen before you reach the tape."

1984

Since Filbert Bayi happened to be in town for the African Olympic Athletes Training Program at Emory, he decided at the last minute to enter the Peachtree. With the incredibly high seed of No. 71, he won in a time of 28:35. Bayi, 31, had the disadvan-

tage of never seeing the entire course before he ran it. He drove the route the day before, but was not allowed to inspect the final half-mile because the park was closed.

After a slow, tactical opening stretch, Bayi pulled away from the field until only South African Ashley Johnson was still with him the last mile. Because he had no idea what lay ahead, Bayi started his kick 200 meters from the park gates and was still sprinting nearly a mile later when he crossed the finish line with a 30-meter lead over Johnson.

Bayi had gone directly to the TV crews without any water. He then said, "Guys, I'm going to go now, I'm dying." Within two minutes, he was back out jogging barefoot in the grass.

Waitz skipped the Peachtree to concentrate on the Olympic marathon, in which she placed second. In her absence, Betty Springs won the women's title. Springs had seen the course backward by car from the airport.

"My main strategy was to go out somewhat easily and pick everyone off gradually," she said. She almost waited too long, however, because she didn't realize there was a woman ahead of her until she found Carol Urish-McLatchie entering the park."

Antonio Villaneuva of Mexico set a world masters 10K record of 29:41 and was 14th overall.

1985

Michael Musyoki led a 1-2-3-4 African sweep as he became the only multiple male Peachtree winner besides Craig Virgin. His second victory came in a course-record time of 27:57.9 as he beat fellow Kenyans Nzau and Simeon Kigen.

"It was like their Olympic Trials right

here at Peachtree," said John Tuttle, who was sixth.

Another African, South Africa's Johnson who had been the runner-up in 1984, was banned from competing in a political move by The Athletics Congress. He voluntarily withdrew to avoid a confrontation.

The Kenyans always thrive on the opening downhill, and they used their front-runner tactics to build the lead.

"When my husband is in his right form, there really isn't anybody who can beat him," said Gloria Musyoki.

Grete Waitz returned to the Peachtree, commenting that the start "was very safe this year." Without a mishap at the start, her time was two seconds slower, 32:02. Judi St. Hilaire was second, 30 seconds behind.

Instead of feeling red, black and blue, like she did when she was bruised and bleeding in 1983, Waitz was red, white and blue.

"The crowd was fantastic, cheering you on," she said. "It felt like a national day, even for a Norwegian."

Francie Larrieu Smith hugs Cathy O'Brien in 1992.

1986

This was a banner year on the course, but not above it. A city ordinance prohibiting banners across the street cost the Peachtree its customary 80-foot focal point at the start.

Irishman John Doherty won the fastest Peachtree of all time with an all-out surge to the tape to beat a former champion and a future champion.

His time was 27:56, while Michael Musyoki was second in 28:00 and Ed Eyestone third in 28:07. The three had been part of an early pack of five, then a trio for the final three miles.

"I thought if it came down to the sprint, I would win it," said Doherty.

At about six miles, it came down to the sprint.

Doherty broke Musyoki's race record by two seconds and his own personal best by 34 seconds.

Eyestone said he'd heard of Doherty, "but I didn't know who he was when we were out there."

Waitz, in severe pain from an injured hamstring, said it hurt so badly she ran the last quarter mile with her eyes closed. "I don't like to talk about injuries after the race," she said, "because I don't like to sound like I'm making an excuse. But since I won, I can tell you that they hurt through most of the race."

This was Waitz's hardest victory. The most she led runner-up Marty Cooksey was 50-60 yards, and she slowed on the downhills because of the pain. In the park, she closed her eyes and imagined herself crossing the finish line. "I was able to keep going," Waitz said, "by telling myself the pain would be over soon."

It was over in 32:10.

1987

Twice a runner-up, Joseph Nzau finally became Peachtree's oldest winner at age 38.

"I count the years like they did in B.C.," Nzau quipped. "Backward."

He had fought injury the previous two years, and his time of 28:34 was among the slowest winning times on the Piedmont Park course. Gidamis Shahanga of Tanzania was second, four seconds later. American Bruce Bickford, a late entrant, was third.

Nzau, who didn't run competitively until he was 23, was the 31st seed, meaning there was no biographical information on him in the press packet.

Outdistancing such big names as Peter Koech, Rob de Castella and Jon Sinclair, Nzau took the lead at four miles and kicked away in the last mile.

"I'm not surprised at all," he said.

Lynn Jennings zipped past Teresa Ornduff as they entered the park to win with a time of 32:22. "She was like a bat out of hell," said Ornduff. "She sat right on my rear end all along, then with a quarter-mile to go, she kicked past me and I didn't have anything left."

Said Jennings, who would go on to win the first U.S. medal in the women's 10K, a bronze in Barcelona, "I consider this a real feather in my cap, and I'm proud to be part of the Peachtree tradition."

1988

A man with a mohawk led the first half mile, but Gerald Lawson was quickly overrun by the field under a layer of fog and fine mist.

J. P. Ndayisenga of Belgium continued the foreign domination of Peachtree by surging past Mark Curp in the park. "It's hard to judge the finish line when you're in the park," said Ndayisenga. "So the best thing to do is to wait until you see the banner somewhere. Then you have about 300 yards left. That's where I made my move."

Curp had tried pulling away at the fifth mile, but couldn't pull it off.

The pair had lost Georgia's John Tuttle and Kenya's Sam Ngatia at Cardiac Hill, where Ngatia was taking water, rare for a world-class runner, but smart in the humid conditions.

"You can't run a fast time," explained Ndayisenga, whose time was 28:17. "You have to run an average time on a day like this."

There was a strong Belgian presence, with Ria Van Landeghem as the women's runner-up behind none other than Grete Waitz, in what has so far been her last Peachtree appearance. Waitz, despite a strained right knee, had a time of 32:10, which gives her four of the 10 fastest marks in Peachtree history.

1989

Both the men's and women's races were won by only a second, with Ibrahim Hussein shoulder-to-shoulder with top-seeded Mark Nenow until the final spurt, and Judi St. Hilaire outkicking Cathy O'Brien.

"I ran scared," said St. Hilaire, who battled a stomach-ache to beat O'Brien 32:05 to 32:06 for the fastest 1-2 finish in Peachtree women's history. "I never was comfortable before or during the race."

It was Hussein's first major 10K victory on the road, and his winning time was 28:13. "When we hit the downhill, I knew I was going to drop Nenow," he said.

Moments before the start, No. 2 seed Keith Brantly decided his turned ankle hurt too much to run, and withdrew from the race. He plopped down in the press truck and cried. "I could have won the race, but I just can't run fast," he said.

O'Brien caught up with St. Hilaire with about a half-mile left, but St. Hilaire had more speed. "She was just more of an experienced 10K runner at the time and was able to outkick me," said O'Brien, who nevertheless set a personal best on the roads by more than a minute. "I was real happy with just being up there."

For the first time, there was drug testing in the Peachtree. The top three men, women, and two random runners from the top 25 in both groups were tested.

1 9 9 0

Dionicio Ceron of Mexico, the dominant runner on the road racing circuit and the top seed, surged just inside Piedmont Park to win with a time of 28:23. Training partner Marcos Barreto, who passed Portugal's Joaquin Pinheiro in the park, was second in 28:27.

Ceron crossed the finish line a good six minutes before the last of the 40,000 runners even started running. The temperature was 73 degrees at the start for the hottest Peachtree since 1983, when runners started in 80 degree heat.

Ceron felt heavy-legged before the race and suffered stomach cramps from the first mile on. Barreto urged him to conserve his energy. "He told me the course was very difficult and not to push until the last mile," said Ceron. "I'm glad I listened to him."

Ceron was the eighth straight non-American winner. "The Americans are very good runners," Ceron stated. "But if you want to win the race, you have to go with who takes the lead. They didn't do that."

John Doherty of Ireland set the course record in 1986, and it still stands.

They did in the women's division. Cathy O'Brien was the favorite, based on her runner-up finish in 1989 and the fact defending champ Judi St. Hilaire couldn't fit the race into her schedule. O'Brien ran away from the field at the three-mile mark, and just missed Waitz's course record with a time of 32:04. At the finish line, she was exhilarated, but also said she felt "relief. I was pretty dead."

1 9 9 1

Finally. Ed Eyestone became the first American since Jon Sinclair in 1982 to win the Peachtree men's division. His winning time was 28:34, five seconds ahead of Mexico's Alejandro Cruz, who nipped

Eeeek! It's cold! A 1978 runner gets sprayed.

Kenya's Steve Kogo by less than a second. William Musyoki, complaining of a sore hip, dropped out at four miles.

"I had that in the back of my mind that it might be nice for an American to win it," said Eyestone.

Eyestone, wearing fluorescent pink, was only the 11th seed, but he was fresher than some of the other guys because he laid out a month after the Boston Marathon due to an injury. "I don't have a great kick, but I'd say it's average," he said. "I can kick with half the guys out there. Fortunately, I picked the right half."

Women's champion Dorthe Rasmussen of Denmark, who had been trying in vain to win this race for as long as an American male, had only one person to outkick: Katerina Khramenkova of the Soviet Union. Rasmussen won by three seconds with a time of 32:42 after it appeared she would lose the race in the final stretch.

Khramenkova pulled alongside at the entrance to the park, and then took the lead by about five meters.

"That's pretty tough when you're leading the whole way and someone passes you in the last kilometer," said Rasmussen. "I felt very tired, but I had to keep going with her. I still had a kick in my legs, and I went for it."

And she got it.

Eyestone gave no guarantees he would return, especially with the heat and humidity. "But the Peachtree is the biggest 10K in the world," he said, "and to be champion of that and set my name up there with the immortals is a good feeling."

1992

One of the grande dames of women's running, Francie Larrieu Smith, floated across the finish line, so giddy at winning that she leaped at the tape.

"Are you kidding? At my age, you can't win races all the time," said Larrieu Smith, who at age 39 set a new course record of 31:49 to break Grete Waitz's mark from 1983. Larrieu Smith, a five-time Olympian who would carry the U.S. flag in the opening ceremonies in Barcelona, found Peachtree was a good preview of the oppressive Spanish heat. "I just was dying at the end," she said, "but I kept saying 'Just keep going, keep going, old lady.'"

In the men's race, Sammy Lelei broke from the pack early and simply wore down every other runner, including countrymen Godfrey Kiprotich and Benson Masya. Lelei was all alone entering Piedmont Park and won by 17 seconds. His time of 27:57 missed John Doherty's course record by a second.

The early pace was blistering, as the lead pack of Lelei, Masya, John Treacy, Kiprotich and another Kenyan, Ezikiel Bitok, covered the first two miles in just under nine minutes.

"A very tough race," said Lelei. "Pace very fast in beginning and it was very hot. I'm happy to win."

Keith Brantly, who was fourth and the top American finisher, said Lelei ran away from the field on Cardiac Hill. "He was too strong. He looked like he could do about whatever he wanted out there."

Larrieu Smith also made her move on Cardiac Hill, passing fellow Olympic marathoner Cathy O'Brien, the 1990 Peachtree champion. "Once I passed Cathy, I was afraid to look back," she said. "I just kept pushing.

"It's a challenging course, but the crowds were fantastic the whole way, and I responded to that."

Curtin, the Peachtree's elite athlete coordinator. "When Osano calls you, you get him in [the field]," said Curtin. "He's a headliner, and other runners accept such a late entry."

Osano won with a time of 28:05, denying fellow Kenyan Sammy Lelei his second straight title.

In the race's first tragedy since 1980, Charles Tutterrow, 40, of East Cobb, collapsed after completing half the race, and was pronounced dead about 45 minutes later. Medical officials said he had arteriosclerosis.

Osano overtook Lelei in the last 300 yards.

"Who is that guy?" one spectator asked as Osano crossed the finish line five seconds ahead of Lelei. "Never heard of him," said another.

Osano had formulated his tactics by watching a videotape of the 1992 race. "I saw Lelei didn't have a finishing kick," he said.

Uta Pippig of Germany pulled ahead at the steep hill just past Brookwood Station and held on to finish five seconds ahead of Anne-Marie Letko. Pippig's time was a relatively slow 32:15.

Francie Larrieu Smith, who in 1992 broke the course record with a time of 31:49 and was seeded first, finished ninth, at 33:49. Larrieu Smith, 40, took the Masters title in her first year of eligibility.

Letko, who pushed the pace while Pippig stayed back, said she was disappointed, but "you can't pout, giving way to the fastest 10K runner in the world this year."

And, added Larrieu Smith, "The beauty of road racing is there's always another race to be run."

1993

Thomas Osano was in Rome—Italy, not Georgia—when his agent called John

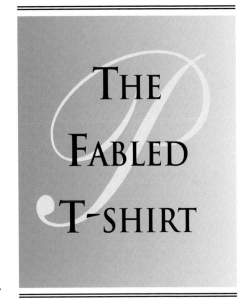

THE FABLED T-SHIRT

It costs more than any ordinary shirt, and money can't buy it. You pay with your sweat.

Of course, we're talking about the fabled Peachtree Road Race T-shirt, and you can trade your sweaty shirt for a crisp new one in the park. You must run the 6.2-mile race in at least 55 minutes to earn the coveted shirt, but don't panic. The time is measured by a separate clock which doesn't start until the last runner crosses the starting line. And nobody checks too closely.

"If they think they deserve a shirt, we're going to give them one," said race director Julia Emmons. "I'm not going to argue with someone who is six-foot-five, and weighs 250 pounds, especially after they've just finished running 6.2 miles."

Emmons usually makes no exceptions for people who didn't run the race, but has been known to give the shirt off her back to a hospitalized runner who couldn't make it to the starting line.

Former race director Bob Varsha says he was "one of the all-time tough nuts when it came to the Peachtree T-shirts." One man sent a letter and photographs testifying he had run a 10K in under 55 minutes on July 4. He didn't get the shirt. The 10K he ran was in Morocco. "He certainly didn't have any Piedmont Hills in Casablanca," said Varsha.

Most people wear the Peachtree T-shirt only once for bragging rights at the July 4 barbecue, pool party or Braves game. Then they tuck it away or make a quilt out of it.

One man took his T-shirt home, placed it on the mantel and installed track lighting to spotlight it. He never ran Peachtree again.

Another proved you can take it with you. He was cremated in his shirt.

Bill Thorn, Sr. of Peachtree City, the only man to have run every Peachtree Road Race, said most of his shirts have never been worn. "It just wouldn't seem right to put on such a hard-won shirt to wash the car or clip the dog's toenails," he said.

After his 1980 shirt disappeared in the washing machine, Don Gamel of Stone Mountain stopped wearing them. "They're the only trophy case I have, so I keep them," he said.

The shirts have been woven into the fabric of Peachtree. "Whenever we got a T-shirt we thought it was kind of neat," said five-time Peachtree winner Gayle Barron. "But apparently not that neat, because most of us didn't save our T-shirts. "Of course, she added, "The T-shirts have gotten more attractive, too."

The design of the shirt is shrouded in mystery until race morning, and everybody has an opinion when he sees it. Well,

to each his own. "It's just part of the ritual that it's a surprise," said Emmons, who budgets more for the T-shirts than any other item, about $150,000, and tests them in the wash. "The more you surround the Peachtree with rituals and tradition, the richer the experience."

The only certainty is it's gonna have a peach on it. The first Peachtree T-shirts had no peach, only a winged foot which, at the time, was the Atlanta Track Club symbol. They also weren't offered until the second year. The first Peachtree runners were shirtless until 1989, when the Atlanta Track Club finally got them covered. Shirts with "Original 110" on the back were distributed for the race's 20th anniversary.

Race founder Tim Singleton believes the Peachtree was the first race where large quantities of T-shirts were given to finish-

ers, and he said, "Nobody's contradicted me. I'll claim it until somebody comes along."

This much he does know: "It caught on a lot of other places."

Here's how the Peachtree T-shirt has evolved:

1970: No shirt.

1971: Singleton got the idea when he ran the Boston Marathon and saw T-shirts for sale. "Believe it or not, people didn't wear shirts that had things written on them back then," he said. Singleton proposed making T-shirts for the first 125 finishers. That meant 73 people went home empty-handed. Besides the winged foot, the red and white shirts said, Carling Brewing Company and Peachtree Road Race.

Harold Tinsley Sr., in his 1977 history of the race, wrote, "Winners of the T-shirts sporting Carling Peachtree Road Race will some day have a collector's item."

1972: This was the exact same shirt, meaning it had no date. The first 250 finishers won them. There should have been enough to reward the previous year's field with plenty to spare, but 330 runners signed up and about 80 were out of luck.

1973: The same situation resulted as in 1972. The only difference was half the field didn't get a shirt.

1974: The shirt wasn't a hand-me-down, but the race was. The Carling Brewing Company decided to rename the race for its premier beer: Tuborg. The design stayed the same, but the name was different. Still no date. The shirt was given to the first 550 of the 765 entrants.

1975: Same shirt, with 600 lucky wearers, 425 given shirt shrift. This could have been the first—and only—shirt to feature a slogan. Singleton enjoyed Tuborg's advertising campaign, which showed celebrities saying, "I'm so and so and I've got class." So he designed the shirt to say the race name and "I've got class." Just before Singleton placed the order, Tuborg officials told him the slogan had changed to "Tuborg beer is a very good beer." And that's why the shirt stayed the same.

1976: The *Atlanta Journal-Constitution* newspaper became the new sponsor, but only the name and the numbers changed, with 1,200 shirts given out. There were hard feelings among some fairly swift runners when the shirts were gone. Because of the unexpected size of the race, approximately 2,250, there was a backlog at the finish chutes. "We heard all kinds of things about people kicking and tripping and scratching trying to beat out other competitors just to get a T-shirt," said race official Sue Peters.

Thus was the 55-minute clock born.

1977: Besides marking the passage of time with the first T-shirt clock—instituted because of harsh feelings when the shirts ran out—this was the first shirt to carry a date. It also was the first with the peach motif. Less than half of the field took home the distinctive souvenir. There were 3,000 shirts, 4,110 pre-registered runners and 2,400 late registrants. Race day registration was eventually dropped.

1978: Same shirt, but interestingly, no date. This could have been an oversight, since three weeks earlier, the printer had said he wouldn't be able to round up enough plain shirts to print. Fortunately, Tom Aderhold, pre-ATC president, worked for a company that produced Arrow shirts.

Jim Kennedy (right) of the Atlanta Journal-Constitution *displays the first dated Peachtree T-shirt in 1977.*

He cleaned out the warehouse. As a concession to the heat, the T-shirt clock time was changed to 60 minutes.

1979: The 10th anniversary shirt was special, with a bold design produced in a contest. However, race director Bob Varsha said the first shipment of shirts was a "shoddy shadow of the prototype," and he demanded revisions. He then wondered if the shirts would arrive. They did. "People don't know how close we've come sometimes to not having those T-shirts in the park on race morning," he said. Because of 2,000 entries the night before, officials ran out of large and extra large.

1980: The shirt reverted to its old design, a simple peach on a white background, because, said Varsha, "the feeling began to surface that this was a valuable trademark to be protected."

1981: The peach was the same, but the color was revolutionary: Peachtree deviated from white to beige.

1982: Back to white. The lowest reliable bidder was in Tennessee, and he didn't realize the deadline pressure he was under. "'Sometime soon,' was not good enough," said Varsha. A convoy of ATC board members and friends took a field trip to Tennessee and came back loaded with the 28,000 shirts. Former shirt director Dick Lusso said there were three stolen shirts. "I can't imagine why anybody would want a T-shirt without running in the race," he said. He then chose his volunteers carefully. "They're all runners, and one runner can tell if he's looking at another runner."

1983: Yellow. Yuck.

1984: People who lived out in the country said they were becoming targets while they ran on the road wearing the shirts. The reason: Peachtree's concession to sponsorship, a big BMW logo on the back of the ash-grey shirt. Some people loved it, others hated it.

1985: Peachtree officials admitted they ran out of shirts, and vowed to have more within two weeks. This shirt was meant to be silver, but looked gray and dull. A more original design adorned a T-shirt nobody got, thank heavens. Crawford Long Hospital made up 20 special Peachtree T-shirts because most Peachtree patients seemed more concerned over not getting a T-shirt than they were over their physical condition. "It does not take the place of the prized Peachtree Road Race T-shirt, but we hope it eases some of the pain," said Dr. Daniel Beless, who nevertheless had no patients to give them to.

1986: The real shirts were blue. A Norcross firm designed a consolation prize, a pale yellow T-shirt with a silk screen peach and the words, "I didn't run '86."

1987: Appropriately, peach colored. This remains one of the most popular shirts.

1988: This year, the big ol' peach shrank, and the peach-colored word Peachtree took center stage on a green shirt.

1989: The "Peachtree at 20" anniversary shirt bowed to tradition and was white, but featured an eight-color design of a runner and a 100-percent-cotton composition. The material was applauded, but the design drew complaints.

1990: This shirt was even more of a departure from the tried and true. The Atlanta skyline, Peachtree Road and peach trees were pressed against a blue background.

Mark Stephens of Alpharetta wrote the *Atlanta Journal-Constitution*: "The Peachtree Road Race T-shirt stinks. Last year's was awful, but this year's is even worse." But Nancy Agro of Atlanta wrote, "The shirts for this year are beautiful, and I am proud to wear mine."

1991: The word Peachtree practically leaped off this shirt. It was gray-toned with purple lettering. Runners were also in high cotton when the Atlanta Committee for the Olympic Games decided to sell commemorative shirts—or singlets—with the Atlanta

Olympics logo on the front and a Peachtree Road Race design on the back.

Only runners with race numbers could order the shirts, and ACOG hoped they would wear them during the race as a "massive visual demonstration," according to ACOG president Billy Payne.

But Emmons cautioned, "This isn't the shirt, it's a shirt. The Olympic shirt is special, but THE shirt is sacred."

1992: A busy, orange shirt showed only the top of a peach, but the word Peachtree twice.

1993: The whole peach was back on a blue background.

1994: The design is secret, but Emmons has already ordered 26,000 extra larges, 20,000 larges, 4,500 mediums and 350 smalls. Race officials have no intention of running out of the larger sizes, which used to happen on occasion. "You only have to run out a couple of times to learn your lesson," said Emmons, adding that the bigger, the better seems to be a safe shirt philoso-

phy. "It took us 10 years to figure that out."

Rob Barge, the *Atlanta Journal-Constitution* graphics designer who designed the last three shirts, said he's "seen people literally throw themselves over the finish line. Most people are tired. They look at it [the shirt] as if they don't care. They stuff it back in the bag. Then the chin goes up and the chest goes out. It's like they say, 'There, I've got it.'"

Jack Pearce got one, lost it, and got it back. He was wearing a Peachtree shirt the day he was hit by a van while running in Valley Forge, Pennsylvania. He spent eight days in the hospital. On his way to the airport, Pearce and his wife stopped by the scene of the accident, and through the mud and weeds found his shirt. Medical personnel had cut it off him.

"I've often wondered what this race would be like if all you got afterwards was to say that you did it," said Pearce. "I think the T-shirt is a big incentive."

RUNNING CLOTHES

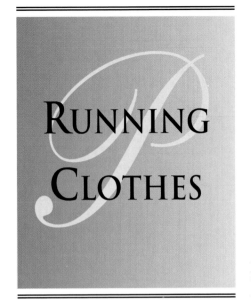

The post-Peachtree dress code bears little resemblance to the way the runners appear at the starting line. In the park, lots of people are, naturally, wearing the same shirt. At the start, participants make individual fashion statements ranging from color-coordinated to rag-tag, comfortable to constraining, bold to predictable. Some just seem to be saying, "I dressed in the dark."

They wear the most expensive running shoes on the market and wingtips. Izod shirts and singlets supplied by running clubs. Bicycle pants and blue jeans. Gym shorts and sweat pants and gym shorts worn outside sweat pants. Designer gear and Bermuda shorts. Baseball caps and bee antenna. Old Peachtree T-shirts and no shirts (men only). Union Jacks and Stars and Stripes trunks. Sweatbands and knee braces. Umbrella hats on their head and key pouches on their feet. Tattered shorts and shorts so new they have never been washed. As one runner wearing brand-new nylon maroon shorts ran under the water sprays . . . well, the shorts ran, too. Now she has maroon socks.

The Peachtree has even been won by someone wearing tacky, flowered Hawaiian print trunks. That was Jon Sinclair, the 1982 champion. His agent couldn't believe his eyes. "I just thought they looked rather amusing," said Sinclair.

Costumes, even "charmingly patriotic headgear," are outlawed because people encased in lycra and plastic can run into trouble in the heat. They are unmasked at the start, or sent on their way . . . home.

Let San Francisco's Bay-to-Breakers have its loonies and its centipedes. The temperature is a lot cooler there than the Fourth of July in Atlanta. The Peachtree, said medical director Dr. Joe Wilson, is "a celebration of running, not a celebration of who can wear the wildest outfit or make the longest chain of people." He also worries that people tripping over their clothes could cause an orthopedic nightmare as well.

But the rules apply only to the dangerous, not the ridiculous. Like the guy in a tuxedo carrying champagne glasses in his hand while a man in a suit ran alongside with a boom box on his shoulder. "Look at those guys in suits," said T. J. Grover, yelling to the tired gentlemen, "I bet that was a lot funnier two miles ago."

Other people go for laughs with less discomfort: they express themselves on their T-shirts: "100% Fat Free." "Joggers do it early in the morning and sometimes late at night." "These are my real teeth, too," was worn by an aged sage. "Craig Who?" (circa 1982, after three Virgin victories). Shirts have been a sign of their times. Adidas and Mickey Mouse and "I rode the bull at Gilley's" were cutting edge 15-20 years ago.

They gave way to "Just Do It" and Bart Simpson. Everybody has their favorite, because most of the people in the funny shirts go slow enough for bystanders to read them.

In the Peachtree's infancy, the only clothes rule was wearing a shirt to satisfy sanctioning guidelines. The first Peachtree champion, Jeff Galloway, recalled wearing a well-used pair of Tiger Cortez training shoes, nylon shell shorts ("considered state of the art at the time"), and an old nylon tricot singlet.

"It was the first nylon tricot I had ever seen and it was soft but very hot," said Galloway. "In *Track and Field News* I had seen the European designs that had straight bar patterns across the midriff. I liked the simplicity of that." So he had his mother sew a bar of red material across the shirt.

The first women's champion, Gayle Barron, wore cut-off blue jeans, and "an ugly tank top I picked up at Penney's. It was the only thing I could find," she said. "I knew I didn't want to just wear a big old T-shirt."

And on her feet? "Quite frankly," admitted Barron, "I think I ran in Keds. Now all these high-tech shoes cost $150, and they wear out faster than the shoes we used to wear. I don't remember having any serious injuries in those godawful shoes."

Bob Manning Sr., who has run almost every Peachtree, is shown in early photos wearing regular Oxford shoes. He said he wanted to be sure he was a runner before splurging on running shoes.

"Fashion," said Barron, "was the least of our thoughts. We never looked around, 'Gosh, that person looks ridiculous.' We were out there doing something stupid as far as everybody else was concerned."

Barron said critics of running used to laugh at her and make horrible remarks. "They'd say 'You're going to be so unfeminine. You're going to ruin your body.' The more they said, the more I put ribbons in my hair and tried to look feminine." The ribbons matched her outfit.

In her first Peachtree, race director Julia Emmons placed second in the women's division but won no sartorial prize. It was 1972 and she wore a polyester blouse and polyester tennis shorts and four-year-old running shoes with the upper leather cracked from age and thin rubber soles nearly worn through.

Galloway said he never saw anybody in street shoes, but some misguided soles were encased in moccasin–type shoes. "They were thinking that the lightness would help, and wound up with brutally bruised feet at the end," he said.

When the race expanded from 1,200 to 12,000 from 1975–78, some of the newcomers turned up in Frank Shorter designer running gear and veteran runners sneered at people in pom-pom socks. Others wore sweatshirts and rubberized shirts to lose weight. "That was totally contrary to everything we were preaching in clinics and newspaper articles," said Galloway. "Folks decided they thought they knew better than that, that they could lose a lot of weight by sweating it off." Many were in worse shape health-wise by the end of the race.

While runners have become brighter, so have the colors they choose to wear. Spectator Todd Neathawk called the passing parade "a sea of Day-Glo. You could turn off the lights and this race would glow in the dark."

Women, of course, always glow. They don't sweat. To prove this point, socialite Sally Danner planned to run the race in hairspray and red lipstick—humidity allowing. "I may not be that cute on the day of the race," she said.

That wouldn't matter. The only appearance that counts at Peachtree is showing up. Then it's time to run. After experiencing the Bay-To-Breakers, Kirk Montgomery said of Peachtree, "At least in this race, I won't look around and see somebody with no clothes on."

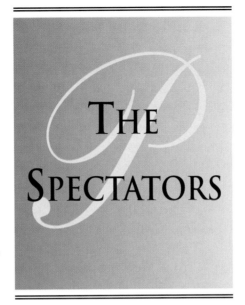

The Spectators

They are on the roofs and the sidewalks, spilling onto the streets or just spilling their drinks.

They play the themes from *Rocky* or *Chariots of Fire* at eardrum-rattling levels, deliver high-fives and chant, "T-shirt, T-shirt," to the weary.

Sure, running 6.2 miles in the blistering heat is tough, but it also takes a lot of energy to stay in one place and watch the race go by.

Let's hear it for the spectators. An estimated crowd of 250,000 line the Peachtree route and pack into the park, armed with lawn chairs, coolers, hoses, signs—"Think Snow," "See Daddy Run. Win, Daddy, Win"—and lots of time. Kids with water balloons take target practice on struggling runners.

Some hoses and sprays set up by spectators have drawn complaints from scantily-clad women, unwilling entries in a wet T-shirt contest.

In Buckhead, the business establishments consider Peachtree day on par with St. Patrick's Day. "We start at about 5:00 a.m. with biscuits and Bloody Mary's on the roof," explained Warren Bruno, owner of Aunt Charley's, the first traditional race landmark runners hit in Buckhead.

In 1982, a topless girl on the roof of Aunt Charley's caused a chain reaction collision when about 300 runners stopped for a closer look that backed up runners for two blocks.

There's usually no water at these watering holes, but runners aren't too thirsty by that time since they've only been running about a mile. Patrons of one Buckhead bar, however, have had a surprise for those whose mouths were dry. Official-looking dixie cups on a table held, not water, but half-hotdogs and pieces of pizza. At 8:00 a.m., who's hungry for that?

The most famous hangout along the route throughout most of the 1970s and 1980s was Harrison's, which had Bloody Mary specials "and every character in the world in front of it," said columnist Ron Hudspeth. Harrison's closed in 1987 and Mick's has now assumed that location at the middle of the Piedmont Hill climb.

Not only was Harrison's at the Peachtree the halfway point, but more importantly in the race's formative years, it was open. "It was a fun day," said Jack Loersch, who was the manager. "There were a mix of people: some who had been up all night, some who got up to watch the race, and some who would only run half the race and stay there."

The drinking establishments along the course all have their gimmicks. One year Loersch offered anyone who won the coveted Peachtree Road Race T-shirt his first draft beer for a nickel. Anyone who didn't

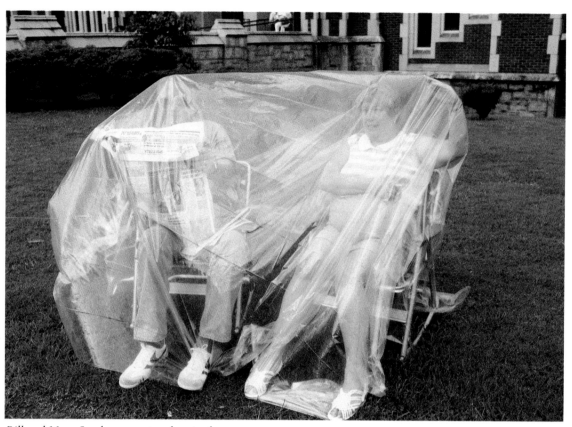

Bill and Mary Sands are wrapped up in the race.

run it got the first *two* for a nickel. Said Loersch, "Those exercised better judgment." He had plenty of takers, but not enough to lose his shirt.

The Acme Bar and Grill serves food only on July 4, lowering the barbecue grill from the rope tethering it to the ceiling. "We ad-lib every July Fourth," said bartender Bill Atherton. "The only thing you can count on is that our owners will open early and after a few drinks they'll try to join the runners in the street."

Well, if you can't beat them . . . heckle them.

Up on the deck at McNeeley's Grill and Bar, one year a man shouted, "If you'd run faster you'd be done by now." And when a group of Marines broke into a walk while passing a hardy soul on the sidewalk, he called out "The few, the proud, the slow."

The residents of Brookwood Hills, locked in by the race, were annoyed by it in the Peachtree's early days. Then they started having picnics, and now wouldn't leave their driveways even if they could.

A trio of spectators one year would not have been allowed in the race even if they hadn't retired from running. Rocky, Boo-Boo and Amber were greyhounds wearing their racing colors. "We thought it was a nice twist," said leash-holder Judy Meisner, an owner of Adopt a Greyhound which tries to find homes for racing dogs after they've retired from the track.

"If these people were dogs," said co-owner Carl Viener, referring to the running crowd, "the first few hundred would be kept, and the rest would be destroyed."

Other spectators are more encouraging. One at the corner of Peachtree and 14th Street held up a sign saying, "You Look

Marvelous Darling."

The best way to get a cheer with little effort? "People carrying the American flag," said Kee Carlisle. "Race next to them."

Patients in wheelchairs and gurneys cheer the wheelchair athletes and runners outside the Shepherd Spinal Center.

Cameras click from both sides of the sidewalk. At least one runner carrying a disposable camera stopped along the way to take pictures of the spectators. Another runner yelled "Thanks for coming," and those around him joined in applauding the crowd.

Some Choice Spots to Watch the Peachtree

1. Nikko Hotel: Huge lawn fronts Peachtree and Piedmont.
2. Bar War Zone: Belly up to the bar at Aunt Charley's, Good Ol' Days, Acme Bar and Grill, Frostbite's daiquiri bar, Three Dollar Cafe and J. Paul's.
3. Cathedral of St. Philip: Another lawn with a view where Andrews meets Peachtree.
4. Bar Zone Two: The Mad Italian and Rio Grande Cantina.
5. Top of Cardiac Hill: McNeeley's, Huey's, R. Thomas Grill.
6. The Beer Mug: This is an official hosing station.
7. Pershing Point: MJ's.
8. Woodruff Arts Center: Along the Olympic Mile.
9. Gorin's Diner: At the turn.
10. Campanile Building: The short marble wall is an excellent place to settle in.
11. The finish. Barbara Walker brings a stepladder to the race to watch from eight feet above. Others climb trees. "It's unbelievable," said Kee Carlisle. "The last few people get in and the award ceremony is over. Everybody's packing up. But there's still people yelling for them."

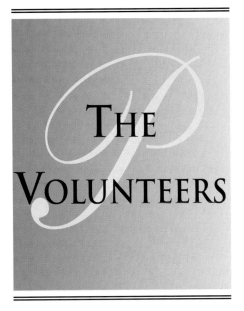

THE VOLUNTEERS

Peachtree Road Race volunteers always put the runners first. Take Lila Brasher, for instance.

Brasher, who has missed only a couple of Peachtrees since 1978, volunteered to videotape the start of the race for the Atlanta Track Club. "It's a real challenge to be able to get down from that 15-story building and start running after everybody's gone," she said. Her goal? "To see how many people I can get ahead of."

Peachtree presses into service about 4,000 volunteers, led by 100 group captains. Some are non-runners; others are runners who have been injured or simply want to participate from a different perspective. They get a shirt, too.

The Wieuca Road Baptist Church, involved in the brouhaha in 1982 when ministers protested the race being run on a Sunday, proved there were no hard feelings by providing 25 official volunteers.

Peachtree takes as much planning as the Normandy invasion. "It's really like moving a small city from one place to another," said Linda Hannon, a former volunteer coordinator.

Volunteers type the names and shirt size of every runner into a data base, put snow fencing in place, time the first 1,000 runners, hand out T-shirts in goodie bags and cart heat-stroke victims into the medical tents. They also fill hundreds of thousands of cups with water and hand them out. If they think a runner needs it, they'll throw the water on him.

The T-shirt bags are packed by disabled senior citizens from the Jewish Vocation Service Senior Adult Workshop. "It's good for their morale because they see that this is something important," said manager Kirk Smith. "They can brag to their friends about it. But it's a lot of hard work. Could you imagine folding 45,000 T-shirts?"

Some of the most popular volunteer positions are almost impossible to land. "For timers, it's like getting tickets to the ACC basketball tournament," said Delores Yaecker. "Somebody has to die and you have to inherit it." A first-place timer named John Bevilaqua almost bit the dust in 1981. He had to run for his life at the start to get on the truck preceding the runners. "I did not get trampled, but I had a fire in my tail," he said. "This sea of humanity came rushing toward me, and I went, 'Uh-oh,' turned and ran towards the truck. The guy in the truck would slow down, and just when I got there, he'd panic and speed up. Somebody stuck their hand out, but I wasn't able to grab his arm. I could see me being dragged along. I yelled to the driver to open the door and dove into the cab of the truck as we hurtled off down Peachtree Street."

For every unforeseen glitch, a volunteer comes to the rescue. Take, for example, the year Peachtree officials asked the city of Atlanta to remove a stop sign in the middle of the road where the race split off onto West Peachtree. Course director Bill Royston was doing a final check on race morning and found that the stop sign was gone, but the metal pole remained. "Nobody told us to do that," said the city workers. Royston and finish line coordinator Bob Brennan pulled out the pole, and Brennan had to run the race with a sore back.

Plans for the next Peachtree begin taking shape the day after the previous race. There are 18 divisions: start area, finish area, signage, media relations, water stations, medical coordination, food, volunteers, invited runners, wheelchairs, communications, course, finish line, registration/results, materials, office staff, technical coordination and race director.

In 1988, it took three times as many volunteers to give out T-shirts in Piedmont Park as it took to put on the entire 1970 inaugural race (no T-shirts were given out then).

Because the start is at the Lenox Square Mall, most of the set-up has to wait until after the stores close. Preparations begin earlier at the finish line. Volunteers must paint the finish line, build a temporary stage, set up a mile and a half of snow fencing and try to ignore Piedmont Park's peculiarities, like the man in the sundress strolling by.

One year, said former race director Bob Varsha, despite security precautions, an unattended car was found parked smack in the middle of the Piedmont Park finish area at 6:00 a.m. "Since no one would confess to owning it, six or eight of us physically lifted it and carried it away," he said. "It was all we could do to keep our volunteers from throwing it in the lake."

Another time, Varsha and some volunteers were out late stenciling the peaches on the mile markers. "A policeman pulled up, hands on hips in the way policemen have, and asked what we were doing," said Varsha. He quickly explained. "Oh, the Peachtree," said the cop. "I've got my entry form right in the car." Then, said Varsha, "he sits down in the street and wants to know why his foot hurts this way as he trains and what he can do to help his foot problem."

Peachtree volunteers are always glad to help.

By the time the trash at Piedmont Park has been picked up, the volunteers will have worked a collective 25,000 hours. And, said Hannon, paralleling the popularity of running the race itself, "We turn people away."

After all of the runners are gone, the volunteers remain to clean up.

First place, Paul Wiggins (left) and finishing second, James Briggs.

lighter, seeking to develop an edge in a race which can be won by fractions of seconds. However, some rules have been enacted to limit the technological advances. "We're trying to keep it a sport instead of a contest between who has the best equipment," said Green.

The wheelchair race has not gone down without controversy.

In 1990, it provided its first official protest in nine years and its two closest finishes. Doug Kennedy, the No. 2 seed from Haleyville, Alabama, crossed the finish line in 21:09.44 to edge 13th-seeded Rafael Ibarra by 45 hundredths of a second. The top four racers were separated by just 1.5 seconds, with third-seeded Jim Knaub third (21:10.29), and defending champion and top seed Blanchette fourth (21:10.94).

All four racers surpassed Blanchette's world record of 21:52, set the year before. Kennedy's three challengers protested, saying he used a thin plastic substance to make his chair more aerodynamic. Kennedy said he placed mylar on the sides of his chair to support his legs.

Trader said the protests were denied

because, "We didn't feel it gave him an unfair advantage."

"I'm shocked Blanchette and the guys would do this to me," said Kennedy, who was paralyzed in a truck accident six years earlier. "I thought I knew them better than this."

Kennedy also registered a complaint, claiming he was impeded when a security vehicle was slow to move off the course about 500 meters from the finish line. He had a 30-meter lead, but had to brake, which allowed Blanchette and Ibarra to go ahead momentarily. Kennedy still won with a surge at the finish.

Blanchette had his best time, but one of his worst Peachtree results. "I'm pretty disappointed," he said at the time. "But this is good for the sport. When you have a dominant figure like myself, it can get boring."

The spectators don't think so.

"It's amazing the number of people who get up half an hour early to watch the wheelchair division," said Green. "I even get letters from people who say they get up for the wheelchair division, then go back to bed (before the footrace)."

73

GETTING IN

The Peachtree experience really begins in March with a race to the mailbox. Since the July 4 event began restricting entries in 1980 to the first 25,000 postmarked applications, inevitably some people have been shut out.

But not shut up. They complained through calls, letters, and appeals through the newspaper. The Atlanta Track Club heard them, felt for them, and diligently figured out ways to squeeze more and more people into the race.

The 1989 Peachtree Road Race reached its 25,000-runner limit just nine days after applications were accepted. About 15,000 people who underestimated the sense of urgency involved were shut out.

"We had 15,000 furious people who wanted to storm the track club," said race director Julia Emmons. "The regulars were lulled into thinking they could get in. We had a number of people who were absolutely sure we had done it to them personally. We knew this problem would not go away."

In an expansive mood, race organizers let in 40,000 the next year. But it ended its practice of sending participants in the previous year's race an application in the mail. Instead, they had to clip their entry from the *Atlanta Journal-Constitution* or pick up the form at official places around town.

The 1991 race closed in 17 days. "It meant that anybody who's at all alert got in," said Emmons, who did allow late entries from about 100 veterans of Operation Desert Storm, but only with a letter from their colonel vouching they were in Saudi Arabia and had no way of getting the applications. Of course, there were still some people left out, but that was their own fault.

"We'll have some pink-faced people pounding the desk," Emmons predicted in 1992, when the race grew to 45,000 and still closed out in 12 days, "but we understand they're mad at themselves and taking it out on us." In 1993, the race closed in an astounding six days.

That was an eternity compared to 1994. The Peachtree, which began with just 110 people in 1970, accepted 50,000 entrants, double its number of years in existence. The first 40,000 places were filled in two days, and were based on order received. An additional 25,000 people vied for the final 10,000 spots in a new Georgia lottery, pioneered by the New York Marathon, among the rest of the applications with March postmarks.

"I hope we haven't made a mistake," said Emmons, "but it seems unfair to not let another 5,000 in there."

Bandits—people who run without a

GONE BUT NOT FORGOTTEN IS THE WORLD'S LARGEST URINAL, WHICH BORE A SIGN THAT SAID, "WE HOPE YOU FIND IT GRATIFYING AND CONVENIENT TO PARTICIPATE IN THE USE OF SUCH A HISTORIC MONUMENT." IT MADE ITS DEBUT IN 1981, BUT WAS FLUSHED OUT OF EXISTENCE 10 YEARS LATER BECAUSE OF THE ABUNDANCE OF PORTA-JOHNS. THE FIRST PORTA-JOHNS ARRIVED IN 1977 (SIX OF THEM) AND NOW THERE ARE ALMOST 500. FOR POSTERITY, A WOMAN ENTERED THE WORLD'S LARGEST URINAL TO TAKE A SNAPSHOT.

number—are scarce at Peachtree. No number, no T-shirt.

They are harmless, however, unlike the other bandits, people who steal numbers. At some apartment complexes, race numbers have been stolen out of mailboxes, prompting the track club to make the packets less conspicuous.

And there is a genuine effort to catch the culprits. "We check the numbers we suspect were stolen against photos taken along the course," said Emmons.

The FBI got involved one year, but on an unrelated matter. Agent George Murray called former race director Roy Benson in 1984 and told him an internationally wanted criminal liked to run. "He had been spied at a few big races and they were hoping he would come to Peachtree," said Benson, who felt it was his duty to hand over a couple of numbers. If that mission wasn't accomplished, another one surely was.

Peachtree shutouts with less clout have concocted some of the best excuses since their dog-ate-my-homework-days.

"I forgot," isn't good enough. How about, "I left it with my boyfriend, and he forgot." The track club's response? "Forget it."

"They are convinced in their heart of hearts that this injustice has been done them, and if they can just tell you their story, you'll let them in," said former race director Bob Varsha. After the deadline one year, he said a man sent in his application with a story of how the post office accidentally returned it to him. "The postmark looked funny," Varsha recalled. "The little circle didn't quite meet. It came around and missed. And it looked like pencil. I took a handful of coins, and sure enough, a nickel fit right over it. I called him. I don't know what made me do this, but I took it as such a personal affront, somebody trying to get into my race, violating my rules."

The man came to the ATC office, and Varsha threatened to turn him in for mail fraud. "He said it wasn't him," said Varsha. "Five minutes later, he came back in and confessed."

Did Varsha let him into the race? "No," he said. "I feel badly about it now. I kind of feel if the guy tried that hard . . ."

Knowing the futility of going to the track club, other shutouts turn to their fellow man. They take out classified ads, station themselves at the escalators outside the Running & Fitness Expo with signs that say "I need a number," go to running stores and rely on word of mouth.

A Louisville, Kentucky disc jockey told his listeners that he would get an official number, although he didn't mail his application on time. He enlisted Mayor Andrew Young's office, as well as his congressman, in his efforts. The Atlanta Track Club tried to bar him for being "rude and obnoxious" in his attempts.

People who realize they're out of town or out of shape are only too happy to part

SIGHTS FOR SORE FEET

*T*he mile signs, ticking off the distance. The sign for mile 3 once whizzed by the start at 4:00 a.m. hanging out of the back of a car. Police got it back. It was hard to conceal the evidence.

■ ■ ■

A female runner who dropped out of the race in front of Huey's, ran into a phone booth, made a credit-card call and then jumped back into the race. "Hey, a long-distance romance," she explained.

■ ■ ■

Love on the run. Bradley Humphries proposed to Regina Buttner while their hearts were in the right place: pumping up Cardiac Hill. Kathy Craig was at the four-mile mark when her boyfriend, Bob Heller, jumped from the sidewalk holding up a sign asking her to marry him. She paused long enough to accept the proposal and kiss her new fiance. "But I had to finish the race," said Craig. "There wasn't even a second when I thought of stopping."

■ ■ ■

A runner blowing "Charge!" on a bugle. How he commanded the wind to do it is a mystery.

---

with their numbers. They paid $15, and can scalp it for $40. Race officials frown on numbers changing hands because those buying the numbers are not registered in Peachtree's medical data bank. There are other problems, too: they often wind up in the wrong time group and Marathon Foto sends the picture of No. 34,567 to the wrong person.

The track club offers people who turn in their unused numbers a guaranteed entry into next year's event, but usually only about 100 people respond.

In most races, 10 percent of the entrants don't show up, but only a fraction skip Peachtree. "People," said Emmons, "just don't miss it."

FIBBING

On the Peachtree entry form there is a little blank for filling in the time you expect to run. This is used for seeding purposes. However, some people consider it an opportunity to be creative.

Runners who can verify a time of 50 minutes or less are placed in the seeded and subseeded groups and time group one. There are approximately 5,000 runners with credentials. The rest determine their starting order by listing a time. Put 50:01, and you might get stuck in the last group. Less suspicious times are grouped accordingly, but people don't always start where they're supposed to.

"In the final analysis, you have to appeal to people's common sense," said former race director Bob Varsha. "If people are going to try to place themselves in the front rank of runners, they're going to be found out."

He has called "the most egregious violators" on the telephone on occasion, telling them that he has their entry form in front of him. "You get that long silence on the other end of the line," he said. "Sometimes it's just an honest mistake. 'I told my wife to fill it in and she didn't know what she was doing.'" Others have heard a four-minute mile is good, so figure they can run a five-minute mile.

On race day, runners can crash the wrong groups by going backwards, never forwards. There are volunteers to see to that. Said John Duddy, in charge of runner control, "We won't chop your head off, but we do ask that the runners line up in the proper groups. If somebody gets out of line we do have the authority to mark their number so they won't get a T-shirt."

Jeff Galloway, the first Peachtree winner, was annoyed in 1987 by the people who jumped in off the sidewalk just past the starting line. "It's a pain to have to wade through them," he said. "At one point I had to weave up on the sidewalk and back."

A snow fence about 200 yards on each side of the starting line helps prevent slower runners from jumping into faster groups. Sometimes the system fails. Two Peachtree participants wrote letters to the editor complaining about misplaced runners. Nancy Agro of Atlanta said the slow runners impede faster ones. "On my application, I wrote that my 10K time is 48 minutes, which is actually the time it took me to complete the race," she wrote. "However, within that group, I found myself dodging people for the first mile and a half. Countless runners did not belong in the group. Not only were there people running so slowly that I could walk faster, but some were walking for the first mile.

"I realize that the Peachtree Road Race is a fun event, and not actually a race as such, but I feel that I should be able to run at my pace to enjoy myself. These people were obviously enjoying themselves because there was no one blocking them. But everyone else who belonged in that group was forced to either weave in and out to avoid them or walk the entire course.

"It is of the utmost importance for the slow runners, and walkers especially, to put down honest times so that they are not hindering everyone else's performance."

Barry Warshaw of Stone Mountain had a different perspective.

"Having, of course, recorded an honest time myself," he said, "I was surprised and puzzled to find so many runners breathing down my neck, nipping at my heels and passing me as effortlessly as if I were walking. At first, I thought that the great cheering crowds and rejuvenating music along the way were distracting me from my best effort. However, growing exhaustion and the expected results on my stopwatch gave evidence otherwise.

"I arrived at the heretic conclusion that many runners must have purposely recorded slower times on their applications just for the pure thrill of passing those of us who were honest."

However, he concluded, "Fortunately, most view the Peachtree as a magnificent and well-organized celebration. Our thrills derive from participating in and completing this unique event."

THE PEACHTREE JUNIOR

The Peachtree Road Race is not child's play.

Getting lost in a jungle of adult legs frightened enough kids that race organizers gave pee-wees their own Peachtree in 1987: the Peachtree Junior.

The 3K race is run on the first Saturday in June exclusively in Piedmont Park. It's primarily for children ages 7-12, but six-year-olds can run if they write a letter asking for permission. A monitor stands by the course every 100 feet offering reassurance if needed.

The first race drew 600 kids who were told that they would always be special, just like the runners in the first Peachtree in 1970.

Munchkins had run the big Peachtree since it began, with five-year-old Terry Thorn among the finishers in 1970. In 1981, six-year-old Greg Sprouie finished in under an hour, and joked about "one guy with humongous legs. I thought he was going to step on me."

As the field grew, so did the number of children, who were not always prepared for the stress of a huge road race. The idea for the Peachtree Junior sprouted from a letter in 1986 to race director Julia Emmons asking if Emmons knew that children were crying in the race. Emmons ran the race that year and found that children were indeed crying. Although some could run the race with less problems than the adults, she talked to pediatricians and decided to set an upper age limit of 10 years old. Children ages 10-12 can run in both races.

The Peachtree Junior is non-competitive, with the youngsters running within their own age group. There's a clock at the finish line if they want to keep time. "We ourselves pay no attention to it," said Emmons.

And all finishers get a T-shirt.

THE ELITE

The first Peachtree winners won fame after they won the race. Now the champions' fame precedes them.

Celebrity runners arrived in 1976, when the Peachtree was trying to boost its profile. Olympian Don Kardong won that race, beating Bill Rodgers, only to lose to Frank Shorter the next year in a field featuring eight Olympians.

"That changed the race," said five-time women's winner Gayle Barron. "That attracted other runners. But now the increase has nothing to do with who's coming to the race. People couldn't care less who's coming. They're running for the fitness of it."

It's still considered an honor, however, to share the road with some of the greatest runners of their time, and of all-time. Mary Decker fell here in 1981 before she fell in the Olympics, tripped by a reflector in the pavement instead of Zola Budd's heel.

Jim Ryun came to run here in 1984 with his son.

Kathryn Switzer, the first woman to run the Boston Marathon (illegally), broke no rules in 1979 when she came just to jog.

Priscilla Welch of England, one of the top masters women in the world, has been an inspiration to fellow runners. "I might look a little worn on the outside," she said, "but the inside is still working well, and that's all that matters."

Jeff Galloway, the first Peachtree champion and an Olympian two years later, said his favorite moment came in 1977 when Lasse Viren accepted his invitation to run. Viren, the four-time gold medalist from Finland, had never run in the United States before. "He was the best," said Galloway, "and for him to acknowledge our race as the only road race he would participate in was a tremendous honor and exciting time."

Galloway finished 10th in that race, staying with the lead group, "until they forgot that I was the one who invited them," he joked. "They had no courtesy at all."

Rob de Castella of Australia was invigorated by the Peachtree atmosphere, but not the temperature. "I'd heard great things about the Peachtree before I came but I was totally unprepared for the turnout," he said. "There was a feeling of celebration in the air. That was the last good feeling I had." He called his performance "dreadful" and promised to come back. "I owe the organizers a better showing," he said.

Peachtree is also the road to becoming a bigger name in the running world. "It's just like Boston," said John Tuttle, a Georgia runner who was third in 1988.

Uta Pippig, a 27-year-old German, crosses the finish line in 32 minutes, 15 seconds.

TRIAL RUN

Other than on July 4, some Peachtree runners set foot on Peachtree Street only to cross it. Others run the course year-round. Sunday mornings coming down Peachtree are runners practicing for the July 4 race. Their numbers swell to thousands as the race nears, making the pseudo-Peachtree the second largest—though unofficial—10K in the state of Georgia.

There's no starter, no clock and no jostling. There are, however, T-shirts awaiting the finishers in Piedmont Park, distributed by local companies. Water stations are also set up along the route, courtesy of the Atlanta Track Club and some generous establishments.

"When I got to Good Ol' Days and saw the water station, my first thought was, 'Gee, I hope it's a margarita,'" said Robert Rombeau. With or without salt?

Most practitioners run the entire 6.2-mile course to Piedmont Park. Others stop along the route and take the bus back to the start. But some turn around and go back, tackling a course more punishing in reverse.

"Somebody told me it gets so packed the day of the race he got really frustrated," said Lisa Chamberland of Morrow. "I can run it today my free-spirit self."

But said Bob Hammond of Atlanta, "It's tough around the churches, with people coming in and car doors opening up. You have to be very careful you don't bang into the doors."

Some runners like to make the race as exact a duplicate as possible. They go through stretching rituals and tap the timing button on their watch precisely at 7:30 a.m.

"My heart rate is already going up thinking about the hill," said Scott King, ready to set out a week before his rookie race. "If you're going to train for it, the best way is doing it. I've heard other people say not to do it before you run it. But I don't have a problem with that."

After Kirk Montgomery runs, he stops in a Buckhead cafe for capuccino and danish, not a breakfast of champions. "It's not good for you," he said. "That's why I run."

Judi St. Hilaire (left) receives a Frabel glass peach from Andrew Young.

"It's not a marathon, but if you do well at Peachtree, it sets up other races for you. People are going to want you to run in their races."

Peachtree wants only contenders, not pretenders. Thanks to Rosie Ruiz's ruse when she took a subway to presumed victory in the 1980 Boston Marathon, Peachtree began assigning escorts to the top women runners to protect the integrity of the race. The escorts enter the race at about three miles and carry flags. Women chasing the leader love it; it lets them spot their competitors.

Ruiz robbed the real Boston winner, Jacqueline Gareau, of the glory she deserved. Gareau ran Peachtree in 1980, but as her escort Greg Sheats tells the story, "She didn't win. In fact she collapsed in my arms in Piedmont Park (about 500 meters from the finish)—but we didn't have any problems."

Lynn Jennings, who made it to the finish line first in 1987, called the race a feather in her cap. "If I wanted to stay No. 1, I knew I would have to win the Peachtree," she said. "The Peachtree is THE road race of the summer."

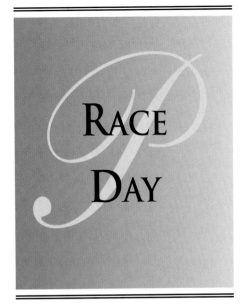

RACE DAY

GETTING READY

The alarm goes off, and your feet hit the floor for the first steps in a long trek to Piedmont Park and home again.

A piece of toast or a banana are plenty for breakfast. The truly serious eat nothing. "No one has ever starved to death during a 10K race," the race instructions say.

You agonize one more time over wearing the new shoes or the old comfortable ones that might fall apart. You choose the old shoes and cross your fingers.

You then stand nervously in a crowded MARTA station, hoping the train won't be full. Peachtree officials recommend MARTA for convenience and to make everyone think they have lots of room once the race begins.

Some people think it's part of the fun to pack onto the MARTA train like a sardine and inhale the smell of Ben Gay. "You find everyone you know naked on MARTA, well almost naked," said Betsy White. Everyone scrutinizes the race numbers worn by everyone else, gloating at some, pouting at others. "He doesn't look good enough to be seeded." "Ooooooh, an 80,000. That'll be a nice, long walk to the start."

When the train arrives at Lenox Square, runners are met by desperate wanna-bes offering up to $100 for a race number, but it's too late. They're left behind on the journey to the staging areas for each group.

Linda Bailey ran her first Peachtree in 1990 with husband J. Fred. They walked a mile from their home in Decatur to the MARTA station. Then they walked from the Lenox stop to the starting area. Another mile. That was followed by a half-mile walk to the starting line.

"Then we ran the race," said Bailey. Afterward, they walked to the Arts Center MARTA station. Another mile. "On our walk home, I told my husband, next year we are going to get a hotel room close to the start."

Which they did. The Baileys no longer join the commuters on the anxious walk to the start, when nature inevitably calls. The women, except for the most immodest, wait in line at a small recreation area restroom, or wait for the Port-a-johns. The men plunge into the woods, finding a suitable tree or bush before resuming the trek to the staging areas on Peachtree from Wieuca to the Lenox Square marquee.

If you're running late, it's sometimes hard to get to the right place. One man scaled a 10-foot-high chainlink fence, gashing his arm, just to start in the proper group.

Finally, within the staging area, there's more room to panic while chatting about training and watching everybody else

Runners will go to any lengths to start in their correct group.

stretch, jog around or meditate from a yoga position. "Why are my legs heavy? Did I put in the miles? Is there time to go to the bathroom one more time?"

Runners carry aspirin, Advil, cups of water, and other useful items, such as the Singleton Survival Kit. Said race founder Tim Singleton, "It's a sandwich bag with a glob of Vaseline. If something starts chafing, I take care of it."

Volunteers scout the area to make sure no one is doing anything illegal. One year there was this announcement before the race: "No vehicles with wheels of any kind are allowed. No baby strollers. No bicycles. No roller skates. No skateboards. And if I left anything out, none of those either."

The thumping music then stops, and the invocation begins, given by a holy man such as Rabbi Alvin M. Sugarman, one year decked out in blue-flowered running shorts and a fishnet tank top. "May this race deepen our understanding of our common humanity," he said.

Everybody is already standing for the singing of the national anthem.

Time to run.

THE STARTERS

In the Peachtree's early years, the most recognizable faces at the starting line were men used to running campaigns, not races.

They were the starters—local politicians race director Tim Singleton invited "to add some more glitz to the race," he said. "And July 4 is a big day for politicians."

Governor Jimmy Carter, formerly a cross country runner at the Naval Academy, started the second annual Peachtree Road Race in 1971. Singleton knew Carter through his job at Georgia State. "The governor's mansion was fairly new then, and he didn't have to go very far."

The next year, Lt. Gov. Lester Maddox, decked out in red, white and blue, fired

the gun and gave an inspiring speech, which runners remember going something like, "Have a good time and remember, if you lose the race, it's your own damn fault."

Atlanta mayor Sam Massell was the official starter in 1973, sporting a brand new track warmup and shoes. Someone asked him, "Hey Sam, are you going to run?" and he shot back, "I have not yet decided if I am going to run."

The mayor, it seems, faced a reelection contest.

The same voice told Massell, "Well, you'd better make up your mind, because the rest of us are getting ready to leave right now."

The mayor barely made it to the finish line ahead of champion Bill Blewett. Blewett was on foot, Massell in a car.

Massell finally did get around to running—for reelection—and lost.

THE START

The fastest reaction time at the start of the Peachtree belongs to the man who drops his hand in a silent "GO!" and then leaps out of the way as 5,000 runners hit the road.

Hold on, aren't there 50,000 people in the race? Sure, but the other 45,000 must cool their heels until they are summoned —group by 5,000-member group—at approximately three-minute intervals. It'll take some 40 minutes for the last runner to cross the starting line, enough time for the champion to be crowned and give interviews. Not to worry. The T-shirt clock doesn't start until the last runner has toed the starting line.

And to think that in 1977, Bob Manning complained it took 87 seconds just to cross the starting line.

Only a staggered start could keep the immense field, double the 1980s limit of 25,000, from clogging the narrow entrance to Piedmont Park. "We want to let the 5,000 who wish to run fast go, and ask everybody else to fall into the spirit of the event," said race director Julia Emmons. "You actually have a lot more fun if you're in the latter part."

The Peachtree used to begin with a bang. Jimmy Carter, Lester Maddox, Andrew Young and Furman Bisher have all fired the starter's gun. The first was Spec Towns, a 1936 Olympian and Georgia track coach in 1970.

In 1984, race director Roy Benson decided to lend a hand to the start procedure, trading in the gun for the silent gesture. "We didn't want people to hear the report of a gun and start pressing forward," he said. "We wanted them to move when the person in front of them moved."

Benson's action was prompted by Grete Waitz's nightmarish experience a year earlier. She fell, but before she could be trampled, her brother Jan scooped her up. Although scraped, bloodied and bruised, Waitz won in record time.

Three-time winner Craig Virgin said he was never tripped, "but like any other mega-race, we were always conscious there was almost this monster behind us, this energy. You could feel the people start to push forward before the gun went off. Thirty seconds before the race, you would wonder if the officials were in control. I didn't want to get creamed and fall down and run over by 25,000 people."

Neither did Lynn Jennings, running her first Peachtree in 1987. She tapped Margaret Groos and said, "I hate these kinds of races, we could get crushed." Groos replied, "Look behind you." Said Jennings, "There was a barrier there where there were no people at all, so I was happy about that."

Benson also divided the runners into pre-assigned color-coded groups with buffer zones between each group. The invited runners start 15 yards ahead of everyone else, the men on one side and the women on the other. "The first part of every group is competitive," said Jeff Galloway. "They're the Type A personalities who get there early enough so they can line up on the front line."

The highest numbers are in the 90,000 range. Restraining ropes hold the runners back, except for those who raise the rope and go under it, creating what starter Tommy Owens would later call "a stampede effect. Some would say, 'I'm not letting that guy ahead of me.'"

Most people obeyed the rules. This helped eliminate the "accordion" start, in which all runners would start to run at the gun, stretch out a few steps, then get bunched up again. This was despite warnings from the announcer at the start, who cautioned, "Now runners, if you've never run in a race this large before, don't expect to start sprinting as soon as you hear the gun. You're gonna have to shuffle for a while."

The object of the new start was to have runners begin when the space ahead of them is clear, for a safe, fast and smooth start. Said Benson, "We've got to remember there are 25,000 people in their colored underwear on the Fourth of July out there having a good time. Except for about 700-1000 people, this is not a life or death race."

In the mid-to-late 1980s, the lag time between groups was only a minute or two. "We have a fine line," said Owens. "We don't want to hold them too long so they're totally unimpeded. We want some slowing effect, but so everybody will be able to run. Congestion has a calming effect on antsy people. People are pumped and overdo it, and die at the end."

Owens said people would ask him after the race if there were as many runners. They'd say, "We were able to run for the first time from start to finish

Atlanta Journal-Constitution
Peachtree
Road Race
Peachtree R
The Atlanta Journal
THE ATLANTA CONSTITUTION

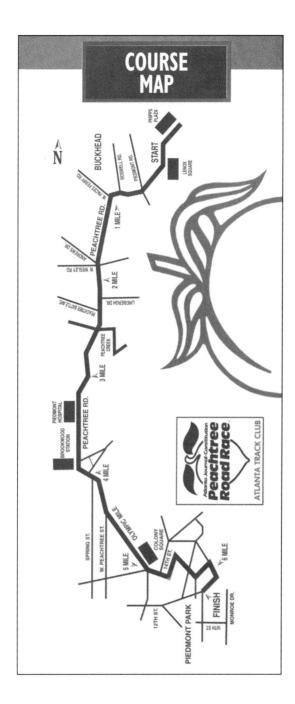

In 1989, Emmons, Grosko, Larry Holder and Bill Royston drove around Midtown looking for alternative routes. First, they thought of running the race down Peachtree to 10th Street, but the finish line would be just past the park entrance. The only entry into the park at this point would be down a steep slope. The finish area crew suggested building a wide earthen ramp into the park to soften the slope. Parks Commissioner Betsy Baker politely wondered if there wasn't another way.

Changing the existing course after the fourth mile would take the runners down West Peachtree to 10th Street, again finishing on 10th. However, this course included some steep hills.

"We thought about putting music at the top of each hill to lull people into thinking it wasn't ghastly," said Emmons.

A roadblock was hit when the engineers discovered an eight-inch curb the runners would have to step up to get into the park. By this time it was mid-May. Desperately seeking a way to expand with a minimum of growing pains, officials introduced the staggered start in 1993— and didn't tell anyone about it. That start was a better-kept secret than the design of the T-shirt.

Nowadays, Emmons personally starts each group, then jumps in with the last one. With the number of people and the buffer zones, the staging area for the back-of-the-packers is all the way back to Peachtree-Dunwoody Road, giving them a nice half-mile warm-up walk.

The groups follow a volunteer holding a sign atop a pole that instructs Walk and Stop. The front line must hold hands to make a natural barrier. "Don't worry, we've got plenty of time," runners reassure each other. By the time the last participants reach the starting line, the top 3,000-4,000 are finished.

But they wouldn't trade places for anything.

without any bottlenecks."

When the field increased to 40,000 runners, instead of changing the start, Peachtree officials originally considered changing the finish. If not, said park coordinator Jack Grosko, "They'd have to just stop at the gate to Piedmont Park and walk through."

THE COURSE

The Peachtree Road Race course of today is a walk in the park compared to the 1970 route. The first Peachtree layout was actually a bit short—estimates put it at about six miles since it was measured with a car's odometer—but it was so brutal it felt like a marathon.

The landmarks where the race started, finished and brought some runners to their knees are no longer in existence. It began next to the old Sears parking lot at East Paces Ferry and Peachtree and ended in Morgana's Fountain. Well, the actual finish was at the Equitable Building, two blocks north of Five Points in downtown Atlanta, but lots of finishers wound up in the fountain named for the Kissing Bandit who took a dip there. It's now a planter. The race began with runners rocketing downhill on Peachtree, then climbing to Pershing Point. At the four-and-one-half mile mark, the course veered onto West Peachtree with a sharp dip, and eventually merged with Peachtree again at an incline that looked like Stone Mountain. There's no longer a Davison's or a Davison's Hill, but next time you drive up Peachtree to Macy's, think of what the hill must have been like before it was leveled off.

Oh, and don't forget the Piedmont Hills. Cardiac Hill, also known as Coronary Hill and Heartbreak Hill, has survived intact, as well as its lesser cousins. Cardiac Hill was the site of intricate defenses by General Johnston during the Civil War, and it is still a barrier.

"Piedmont Hill separates the contenders from the pretenders," said Adrian Leek, who had high placements, but never won Peachtree.

Pioneering Peachtree champion Jeff Galloway said the current course is "dramatically easier" than the one in 1970. "It just kept going uphill," he said. "It was a roller coaster ride from 14th all the way

The old Coca-Cola sign was a welcome sight as runners crested Davison's Hill at 10:00 a.m. en route to Central City Park.

up to Five Points. The new course finishes lower than it starts; the old course finished higher."

Boston marathon champion Bill Rodgers said that "mile for mile, the terrain is more demanding than the Boston Marathon. Boston would be brutal if it were like this all the way."

In those days, said race founder Tim Singleton, "We used to try to make courses tough." He recalled another one of his concoctions, the Peachtree Battle race, and running past a guy who told him, "I wish I could find the S.O.B. who laid this course out."

The Peachtree first deviated from the original course in 1973 when the finish was moved further down Peachtree Street to finish on the left side of Central City Park across from the Trust Company bank. The start was moved forward an equivalent distance. "From year to year, one could not be sure precisely where the finish would be," said Lew Birdseye.

In 1974, there was a slight change when

the course was accurately measured for the first time, and indeed turned out to be short. The start was moved back up Peachtree Road, a few hundred yards south of the Roswell intersection—back to the Sears parking lot.

There was a traffic jam at the finish chute in 1976 when there were many more entrants than expected. The size of the field, combined with the heat and congestion downtown that made the 1977 finish look like a war zone, resulted in the Peachtree course changing substantially.

Kenny Moore, a former Olympian and *Sports Illustrated* writer, suggested to Galloway that the finish be moved away from downtown. He had fond memories of Honolulu Marathon runners streaming into a beautiful shady park . . . like Piedmont Park. Galloway made some calls. Bob Brennan, later president of the Atlanta Track Club and now the man who exhorts runners to "Keep moving" at the finish, told Galloway, "That's a stupid idea. What do you want to do that for?" But Galloway was persistent, and Brennan contacted Michael Lomax, then the city of Atlanta's commissioner of parks, cultural affairs and recreation, about using Piedmont Park. Lomax agreed.

By tracing the route in reverse, the new start line was fixed near Lenox Square. Instead of starting downhill, there was now a slight uphill to Piedmont Avenue. A good segment on West Peachtree remained, and race organizers decided to approach the park from 12th Street instead of at Colony Square and 14th Street. They figured it was better to narrow the field on a street instead of funneling runners onto a slender strip of pavement in the park. Best of all, the last big uphill was replaced by a downhill.

The runners entered Piedmont Park at the American Legion hall, then circled counterclockwise within the park to finish near the bath house. However, the bath house area was cramped, and the transition from wide Peachtree Street to two-lane 12th Street turned out to be difficult.

In 1979, the trek up 14th street began at West Peachtree. That was a truly horrendous hill, past the site of today's IBM Building. The course took runners into the park through the stone gates, wound around the ball fields and curved past the lake and finished near the 10th street entrance.

Craig Virgin remembered a store with a bouquet of balloons outside. "That marked the last hill I had to climb," he recalled.

The next major change occurred in 1982, thanks to MARTA construction which tore up West Peachtree. Instead of Westward Ho! at Pershing Point, it was another long slow climb past the Arts Center, which was only slightly easier than the 14th Street mountain.

The Peachtree has stayed the same ever since. If you're alert, you can spot the mile markers with a number inside a peach painted on the sidewalks.

As the race begins, there's a dip, then a slight incline the first mile, followed by a downward plunge the next mile and a half, particularly steep past Jesus Junction. The course bottoms out at Peachtree Battle.

Then comes Cardiac Hill, a steady climb of roughly 125 feet in elevation spread over nearly a mile of the course. It crests just past Piedmont Hospital.

Though the course has 293 vertical feet in uphill segments, and 400 feet in downhill segments, most of the downhill has been enjoyed by the halfway point, before runners reach the highway overpass. After a brief respite, about a mile of slight downhill past the hospital, they face what course director Bill Royston calls "the stair step," when the course goes uphill, then a little down, then level, then uphill, etc., until the half-mile downhill cruise into Piedmont Park.

Now comes a crucial reminder: there is still one-tenth of the race, more than half a mile, remaining when you enter the park.

"I think Peachtree favors strength people over the speed people," said John Curtin, the Emory track coach who oversees the invited runners. "The race starts out fast because it's mostly downhill, but if you don't go with the pack, you just don't catch up. You have to go out strong and hard, and then you hit the hills."

No matter how tough the race seems, it could be worse. Said race director Julia Emmons, "If we turned it around and finished at Lenox, people would really hate it."

MILE BY MILE

The six miles of the Peachtree Road Race have identities as diverse as the five boroughs of New York in the NYC Marathon. Runners sense the personality changes in mood and terrain, and reflect them in the rhythms they pound with their feet.

Mile One: The first mile is very happy; not just flat, but slightly downhill. The approach into Buckhead is giddy and glitzy. Music is blaring and your runner's high is matched by the intoxication of the people outside and on top of the bars.

Mile Two: You're probably going as fast here as you're going to go. The stretch from Jesus Junction to Peachtree Creek is so steep you can hear the wind rushing by your ears. Ain't gravity wonderful? But don't overstride. Now warmed up, you're talking and laughing as you pass exclusive high-rise apartment buildings. There is a lot of breezy interaction with the crowd.

Mile Three: Whoaaaa. At about the 2 1/2-mile mark, the first hill looms. It's going to be okay, but the chattering quiets to an uneasy murmur. Is the last digit of the

population sign at the Darlington really blinking, or is it just me? The patients at Shepherd Spinal Center offer encouragement, but passing Piedmont Hospital is the toughest part physically and psychologically. This is where the leaders make their breakaway moves, but the object for most is to conserve and survive.

Mile Four: Relief mixes with trepidation as runners are more attuned to water stations than the next round of watering holes. Cardiac Hill is over, but the next hill is more subtle, so you can't figure out why you feel so bad. The stretch after the Beer Mug is the dullest part of the race, and the upward climb over the highway with no shade doesn't help.

Mile Five: The Olympic mile is a sight to behold. Coming over a slight rise, you see thousands of bobbing heads moving steadily forward and water cascading in sprays across the foot traffic. Atlanta '96 banners are up, the Olympic fanfare is playing and you feel like you can conquer the world, or at least this upcoming hill. They don't call it the High Museum for nothing. Funny thing is, it doesn't look like a hill until you're on it.

Mile Six: You're tired, but beginning to feel elated. Your shoes are wet. Is that a blister forming? But you're gonna make it. Here's the last water stop, so drink up. The crowd is thicker by Colony Square, and you round the corner and head *downhill.* Smile for the Marathon Foto cameras as you get ready to burst into the park. Don't be deceived, though, because there's more than half a mile to go. Whoaaaa (Part Two). You're in the park, you've earned that respect, but the crowd has tightened and there's little room to maneuver. The chant "T-shirt, T-shirt" imbedded in your conscience, you try a finishing kick. That's fine for the leaders, but it offends the back-of-the-packers. You should have used that energy on Mile Two.

Mile Six and Change: An eternity. It's

flat, but seems like uphill. You pass through a corridor of faces. They cheer wildly, "You're almost there."

You're there.

THE FINISH

"It looks," says Bob Brennan, "like a dam breaking. First you see one skinny guy, then a couple more skinny guys." And then, whooooosh! For the next hour, skinny and not-so skinny guys, gals and folks of indeterminate gender flood across the finish line in Piedmont Park.

Brennan should know. He is the finish line announcer, standing high above rush hour. He congratulates the runners, directing them left or right, but always to "Keep moving" and "Put your arms up in the air."

The finish line is painted on the pave-

ment and indicated by an overhead banner. There are two big digital clocks. The one on the left is the official time. If you weren't keeping time with your own watch, your race time is the official time minus the minutes it took you to reach the starting line. The clock on the right is the T-shirt clock. If it hasn't reached 55:01 by the time you get there, you will have officially earned your T-shirt. The T-shirt clock does not begin ticking off the minutes until the last runner has crossed the starting line, proving that old adage: It's not where you start, it's when you finish.

Before Brennan became the public address announcer, he ran the race. One year after he finished, a race official tried to press him into service. He said, "How about standing here and as soon as the clock hits 55 minutes, direct them that way." Brennan replied, "I'm not going to stand here and tell these people they're not getting a T-shirt."

Now he tells them they are. "I know the people who come in at the end are most appreciative of any encouragement they get," he said. "They've been out there longer than anybody."

The first across the line are the wheelchair racers, who start half an hour before the runners. The wheelchair record is the world record time of 19 minutes, 58 seconds, rolled by Paul Wiggins of Tasmania in 1993.

The wheelchair racers are still bearing down on the finish when Brennan announces that 6.2 miles away, "The Peachtree Road Race is underway." A cheer goes up.

It's up to the PA announcer to keep the Piedmont Park crowd up to speed on developments. The job has had some rough spots, like the time an announcer who preceded Brennan said, "We've got the wheelchair finishers and I'm going to run down a few of them right now."

Oops. The announcer stays in walkie-talkie contact with the lead vehicle. Peachtree has been won in as little as 27 minutes 56 seconds (John Doherty, 1986), and as much as 32:22 (Jeff Galloway, 1970). There are no official times after the first 1,000 runners.

It's not hard to figure out when the leaders are in the park. One year the announcer was drowned out by five helicopters converging over the lake to film the leaders. "I think we're under attack," he said.

A few minutes later, the true invasion began. At 36 minutes, "the bubble" comes through, and it looks like it will never stop bursting. To add to the congestion, the finish area is already swarming with spectators, officials and mounted police.

"We have to have someone up above who can see and direct the flow of people, 'Go right. Go left,'" said Brennan. "It's almost like playing with faucets. You turn one up and one down."

Under the old system, in 1981 some veered left and found themselves on the other side of a temporary fence from the T-shirts. The fence, naturally, never stood a chance.

One finish line story has been cleaned up since it happened. It's the one about the mounted policeman's horse, which got scared about a minute before the leader appeared and . . . plop, plop.

"It was a fight or flight thing," said Penny Kaiser of the Atlanta Track Club. "We had 25,000 people who were going to be stepping on that."

She jogged out with a newspaper and picked it up. "That's not an assigned job," she said, "but somebody's got to do it."

Thus, their soles were saved.

The medical corps saves their bodies.

Announcements telling runners to put their arms up in the air give the volunteers a subtle way of finding out who's paying

Andrew Young was a familiar sight at the Olympic Mile in 1989. "Everybody who ran by wanted to slap palms, and see how hard they could slap."

attention, and who's disoriented and suffering from the heat. Also, said nursing coordinator Cindy Brown, "The nurses know to look for people who are weaving, glassy-eyed and wandering off course."

There are three medical pavilions stuffed with cots, ice, and depending on the temperature, people.

The vast majority of runners don't need medical assistance, and many immediately head for the huge sprays to get relief and even relieve themselves. The spray was the site of the famous "Battle of Atlanta" photograph.

Dips in the lake are not allowed, and frogmen waiting in rowboats are there to enforce the ban.

From the drenching water, it's on to the Crystal Springs drinking water. PowerAde, Coca-Cola and La Croix sparkling water are also provided.

Then runners line up one more time for the T-shirt, grabbing their bag of goodies while a volunteer scrawls a big X on their number. One year, besides the shirt, the bag contained a strawberry cereal bar, fruit chews, a note pad with the Atlanta Track Club schedule and a box of Uncle Ben's Converted Rice. Just add hot water.

Another freebie is a massage provided by students of sports massage. There's a time limit, however.

As hot and sweaty as the race is, the park is even steamier as people wander around looking for friends and family or stand under the alphabetically arranged balloons near 10th Street. There is also a missing persons booth up the hill away from the awards stage.

In 1993, those really going bananas after the race ate a fruit treat provided by a gorilla. Donning the hot and hairy suit was Anne Taylor of Norcross, a marketing representative for Texaco, which provided the bananas. "I'm telling people that I won the race—first place in the animal division," she said. She also said she had a couple of men "come up to me and say, 'Dear, I've been looking all over for you,' like I'm their wife."

Runners and their real families sprawl on the grassy hill or sit near the stage where a band entertains and the awards presentations are held. "They'll stay for the awards ceremony out of curiosity," said Brennan, "to be awed by the fact these people ran this sucker in 27 minutes and change."

The post-Peachtree celebration is another place to renew old acquaintances and start new ones. Ken Bedelle and Alan Pilling gather for a party with fellow members of the Chattahoochee Road Runners on the hill. "We have been known to be the last to leave the park," said Bedelle, who has run Peachtree since 1977. "We stay till it's over with."

The party picked up and moved to the Limelight nightclub in 1986 and 1987 for the "Cool Down with Craig Virgin." About 600 people came the first year, 800 the next for the party, which raised $1,200 for a Piedmont Park running trail. "They drank beer and fruit drinks, and seemed to get over their kinks and recover from the race," said Virgin. "They were dancing on the speakers. That was the cleanest crowd that ever crossed the threshold of the old Limelight."

PRIZES

T-shirts are not the only prizes awarded at the completion of the Peachtree.

Specially-designed Frabel glass peaches, in which the cleft and leaves resemble the hills and curves of the course, are awarded to the top 20 men, top 10 women, top five masters men and women, top wheelchair athletes and the first Georgia man and woman.

The purse is $50,000, with an additional $1,000 awarded to the man or woman breaking the open division course record.

Athletes who aren't quite world class can win smaller sums by beating certain times.

In the first Peachtree in 1970, the winner's trophies had a little brass-plated man on top. Gayle Barron got the same trophy as Jeff Galloway.

Then the winners received plaques and the top five finishers in each age group earned trophies.

Peachtree awards have since gained a certain measure of notoriety on their own. For a few years, a local artist named Mary Allen produced leaded stained glass pieces with a different theme each year.

Winners also received glass trophies of runners or a 2x2-foot wooden peach before race organizers decided to stick with the glass peach. The first Georgians have won an Apple computer, as well as an invitation to be part of the Olympic torch run through Spain in 1992. Nike added to the pot in 1993 by giving ceramic mementos to the first 1,000 finishers.

One of the best prizes required another giant sprint. In the early 1980s, Wolf Camera sponsored a race to their 10th Street store. The first runner to arrive with a Wolf Camera hat, Peachtree number and T-shirt won a $1,000 savings bond. It wasn't a photo finish. According to Lee Fidler, Benji Durden won (he ran), Jeff Galloway was second (he was driven) and Fidler reached the store somewhere in the Top 10. He and Galloway won cameras for their effort.

And they still had the T-shirt, too.

CHARACTERS

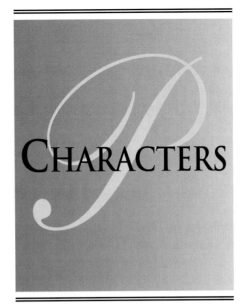

You've gotta have character to run the Peachtree Road Race, but some runners would rather be one.

Some are obvious, like the joggler. Bill Giduz has kept three balls and himself going for 6.2 miles—a real juggling act.

Eddie Young ran the 1984 race barefoot in 37 minutes, 22 seconds. And that was pre-Zola Budd.

Then there was the Phantom of Peachtree, a man who wasn't intoxicated with running. He was intoxicated while running. According to local legend and Ron Hudspeth, the Phantom, who once downed 77 beers at one sitting, stayed up drinking the night before Peachtree. At daybreak, someone bet him $100 he couldn't run the race. The Phantom had been a pretty fair college athlete in his day, so he jumped in his car and drove to Buckhead. He didn't know the race started at Lenox Square.

He started running in his street clothes with his pants rolled up, and didn't know if he was ahead of the pack or behind. He was ahead, but not for long. "I looked back and you wouldn't have believed the mob that was coming at me," he told Hudspeth. "Oh my gosh, someone's opened the gates to hell."

Just before the Phantom got to his favorite hangout, Harrison's, the lead runners caught and passed him and he collapsed and fell in the gutter. "One guy remembered seeing him trying to drink water out of the gutter," said Hudspeth. "Then he started running again, and collapsed again around Piedmont Hospital."

The Phantom was whisked into the emergency room on a stretcher. "They said, 'This man hasn't had heat stroke. This man is drunk,'" said Jack Loersch, then the manager at Harrison's. He said he'd only had a bottle of vodka and a case of schnapps.

There's also been an entry for another phantom figure, Georgia Tech's George P. Burdell.

Those who did show up have been superheroes, dead legends, insects and all-stars. Superman wasn't faster than a speeding bullet, and Batman could have used his Batmobile. And then there was the man with 007 on his chest. Bond? James Bond?

A whole beehive has run with little antenna on their heads, and another runner wrapped ivy around his head like he was Phidippides, the first marathon casualty. He survived.

Boog Powell, the beer-bellied former Baltimore Orioles first baseman, was on the press truck one year with a Miller Lite in his hand and sucking on a cigarette.

Tim Monteith carries a torch for the Peachtree as a spectator, but costumes such as his Statue of Liberty get-up are strictly forbidden within the race.

The Boogmeister surveyed the masses at the starting line and pronounced: "Is this bleepin' great or what?"

Some runners draw attention to themselves for noble causes. Bill Lynch of Conyers has run the race backward to "erase backward notions" about epilepsy, which afflicted his son.

Lt. William Ashcroft of Atlanta, a Persian Gulf War veteran, ran in full Army camouflage gear—including boots, canteens and a 30-pound pack—to raise money for a program to assist Gulf War veterans and their families. He had $48,000 worth of pledges.

Others have dubious motivation. One year as the public address announcer intoned, "Here comes the last runner," Rhona Caplan appeared wearing a headset and silver Mercury wings on her shoes and waving an American flag. She then collapsed in the arms of family and friends and gasped to the television cameras, "Thank God for my legs." She said she ran for her father, who had lost his legs.

There was just one technicality. Caplan had finished 15 minutes earlier, and sneaked back out on the course and staged the whole thing in kind of a reverse Rosie Ruiz. "What was I gonna do?" she said. "Tell 'em I didn't finish last?"

IRON MEN

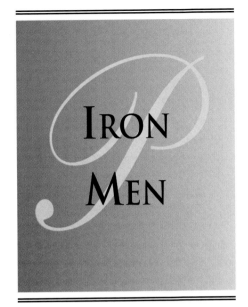

And then there was one.
Bill Thorn Sr. is the Peachtree Road Race's Iron Man. He is the lone survivor of all 24 races, and will be at the starting line for the 25th on July 4. Count on it.

Thorn, 63, of Peachtree City—a perfectly named hometown, although he didn't plan it that way—ran the 1993 race with a sprained ankle. "I just did get through it," he said.

Did it ever cross his mind to skip the race? "No."

Did his family encourage him to skip the race? "No. They knew I'd do it anyway."

Don Gamel, 54, of Stone Mountain, formerly shared Iron Man status with Thorn, but fell by the wayside in 1993. "I hated to miss it, but it gets harder every year," said Gamel, who one year managed to put off an ulcer attack until after the race.

This time a toothache triggered a form of arthritis in Gamel's knee so painful he couldn't run. "I had already sent my application in, but it was just impossible," said Gamel. "I just sat at home hurting."

Thorn had looked for Gamel at the race. In their first Peachtree, the two had been track coaches in East Point and often ran together. Thorn finished 78th among the 110 runners, just behind his son, Bill, and Gamel's son, Chuck, while Gamel, called "Dave" on the official results sheet, was 41st. Terry Thorn, age five, was the youngest entrant, placing 106th. Gamel's daughter, Karen, would later finish second among the women in 1974, at age 10.

The kids were too young to become obsessive about running the race, but their fathers just kept coming back. Thorn ran into race founder Tim Singleton in Piedmont Park a few years ago and Singleton told him, "There's only two or three of y'all left, so y'all keep it up."

Thorn, the athletic director and head football and track coach at Landmark Christian School, said a streak like his takes luck, health and an understanding family. Wife Patty has also run the race on occasion. "You've got to set that time aside," he said. "We plan everything around it."

To Don Clement's eternal regret, his 23-year streak began with the second Peachtree. "If I had only known about it, I would have been there," he said. "I've thought about that many, many times. I was only running two miles, but that wouldn't have stopped me."

Clement runs only in good weather, starting in mid-May and quitting July 4

Don Gamel (left) had to miss the 1993 Peachtree, leaving Bill Thorn Sr. (right) as the only man with every race under his belt.

Don Clement's long-running Peachtree streak began with the second race—to his everlasting chagrin.

THE U.S.S. *ATLANTA* SUBMARINE CREW WORE T-SHIRTS BEARING THE SHIP'S NAME, BUT DID NOT RUN TOGETHER OR COUNT CADENCE LIKE OTHER SERVICE TEAMS. "WE'LL LEAVE THAT TO THE MARINES," SAID ONE. "WE'RE SAILORS."

after the race. "If I'm not training for anything I'm not going to run just to be doing it," he said. On race morning, he drinks a glass of milk. And he never, ever warms up. "If I start doing that, I might mess up my system," he said. And that system has served him well. "I've never walked a step of the Peachtree," he said. "That's something I hold onto. I've never won, understand that."

Neither Thorn nor Clement can imagine missing a Peachtree "That ain't gonna happen," said Clement. "It's part of my marriage contract. The Fourth of July, I haven't been anywhere in 25 years."

Thorn has earned the last word. "I plan to do it until they run me off. Or haul me off. One or the other."

from running. But I didn't want to start a political uprising."

Craig Virgin, a three-time winner, said the athletes favored letting Johnson run. "We knew he was not responsible for apartheid. It was bigger than all of us." But he added, "TAC was trying not to lose face."

The race was won by Michael Musyoki, and Johnson said he wasn't embarrassed to admit he lost a lot of money. Tenth place was worth $400, and he had earned $3,000 the year before with his second-place finish. However, he said, "I don't think I lost out in my stature as a runner. I gained."

At the awards ceremony, Aderhold introduced Johnson and said he couldn't run because he was South African. There were boos from the crowd. "I couldn't believe it," said Johnson. "I was shocked. These people are actually on my side. The support was for me. Nobody's said, 'We're glad you were banned, or had to withdraw.'" Johnson took the microphone and thanked the track club for its support, and for inviting him back the next year.

The situation inflamed public opinion, with letters to the editor supporting both sides of the issue. Dr. Julian Bond, then a state senator, wrote that he thought Johnson's civil rights had been violated and he had grounds for a lawsuit. "Discrimination is just that, no matter where it takes place or to whom it happens, and especially when it is an open sporting event. Johnson was acting as an individual and not as a representative of any foreign country or any organization."

Others wrote to commend TACs intent "not to hurt or make martyrs of South African athletes, but to call attention to their country's discriminatory policies of racial segregation."

Atlanta mayor Andrew Young said it was "unfair, but we're talking about a country that deprives people of their rights based on race."

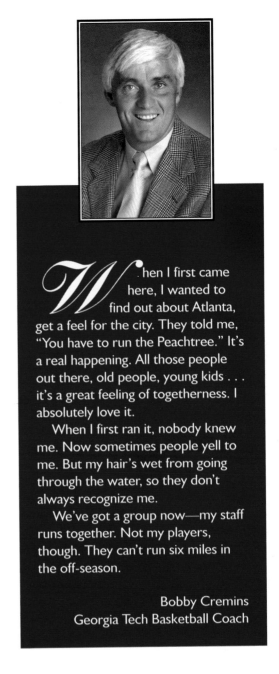

*W*hen I first came here, I wanted to find out about Atlanta, get a feel for the city. They told me, "You have to run the Peachtree." It's a real happening. All those people out there, old people, young kids . . . it's a great feeling of togetherness. I absolutely love it.

When I first ran it, nobody knew me. Now sometimes people yell to me. But my hair's wet from going through the water, so they don't always recognize me.

We've got a group now—my staff runs together. Not my players, though. They can't run six miles in the off-season.

Bobby Cremins
Georgia Tech Basketball Coach

A letter to the editor called it "a national disgrace for our city," and another asked, "What right do we have to trample on this person's human rights?"

That's what the ATC wanted to know, too, and later met with TAC to discuss its relationship with the governing body. The differences were resolved, and Johnson ran in 1986, but did not crack the Top 12.

THE PEACHTREE ROAD RACE FROM A TO Z

A is for Application. Get it in quickly.

B is for Blisters. Ouch.

C is for Cardiac Hill. Ya gotta have heart.

D is for Distance. 6.2 miles—or 6.7 from the back of the pack.

E is for Exaggeration. Now *how* fast did you run?

F is for Flags. Lots of them. It's the Fourth.

G is for Galloway, Jeff and Gayle Barron. First in the first.

H is for Harrison's (August 8, 1974 to January 1, 1987).

I is for Invited Runners. They finish before some of you start.

J is for Jesus Junction. Pray for cloud cover.

K is for Keep Moving. The soothing words you hear as you finish.

L is for Large. Or X-Large. Most Peachtree shirts.

M is for MARTA. Take it.

N is for Numbers. World's largest 10K, 50,000 this year.

O is for Overpass: I-85 is below. The traffic's up here.

P is for Peeing in the bushes. Be discreet.

Q is for Quiet. The hush before the start.

R is for Rocky. Somebody, somewhere will be playing it.

S is for Squishy shoes. Inevitable.

T is for Temperature. It's gonna be hot.

U is for Underfoot. Cups, cups, cups.

V is for Volunteers. There'd be no race without them.

W is for Water Sprays. Go under them. See T and S.

X is for that big black mark on your number when you get your T-shirt.

Y is for Yonder. Where you parked the car.

Z is for Zoom. Wheelchair racers going downhill.

PUTTING ON THE PEACHTREE

By the numbers, the Peachtree Road Race is 100,000 feet covering 32,736 feet. If every runner stood shoulder width apart, there would be enough people to reach the finish line, go back to the start, and then almost to Peachtree Battle again.

According to Brantley Sherrer of the Atlanta Track Club, on race day, the Peachtree requires:

490,000 cups
50,000 runners
26,000 extra large T-shirts
20,000 large T-shirts
15,000 gallons of water, pure Crystal Springs plus good old Atlanta water
12,100 feet of snow fence
4,500 medium T-shirts
4,000 volunteers
4,000 pounds of ice
3,200 safety pins.
2,000 towels
1,920 gallons of Power Ade
1,500 liners for trash cans
1,300 stakes
1,000 index cards
1,000 pull ties
500 trash bags
456 tables
420 trash cans for trash
400 feet of cable
400 feet of rope
379 portajohns, 5 handicapped
350 small T-shirts
324 trash cans (to hold water)
250 sawhorse barriers

234 chairs
200 feet of flagging
200 feet of rope
200 traffic cones
150 Red Cross singlets
112 rolls of engineer's tape
111 hoses
80 bull horns
70 cots
60 plastic sheets
50 red hats for stretcher bearers
40 stretchers
34 walkie-talkies
32 rakes (to rake up cups)
30 water pitchers
24 helium balloons to hold up various banners
20 rolls of duct tape
20 poles with nails on end to pick up trash
15 wire cutters
12 clipboards
10 cases of Power Ade in cans (medical)
10 cases of Coke (medical)
10 watches for timing vehicle
9 tents
7 gallons of highway marking paint
6 24-foot trucks (5 just for T-shirts)
5 100-foot electrical cords
5 golf carts
5 15-passenger vans
2 14-foot ladders
2 clocks
2 bucket trucks
2 staplers
2 finish line poles
1 finish line banner

THE STATS

RACE START TIMES

1970	9:30 a.m.
1971–77	9:00 a.m.
1978	7:00 a.m.
1979–81	8:00 a.m.
1982 (Sunday)	7:30 a.m.
1983–92	8:00 a.m.
1993 (Sunday)	7:30 a.m.

RACE DAY TEMPERATURES (AT START)

Year	Temperature
1970	80°
1971	70°
1972	70°
1973	80°
1974	71°, rain
1975	72°
1976	68°, foggy
1977	80°
1978	73°
1979	76°
1980	80°
1981	69°
1982	75°
1983	80°
1984	72°
1985	69°
1986	62°
1987	68°
1988	65°, foggy
1989	62°, foggy
1990	70°
1991	80°
1992	77°
1993	74°

SIZE OF THE FIELD

1970	110 finishers (3 women)
1971	198 finishers (4 women)
1972	330 finishers (17 women)
1973	525 finishers (12 women)
1974	765 finishers
1975	1025 finishers (approx.)
1976	2,250 finishers (approx., finish cards ran out at 2,032)
1977	6,500 entrants (2,400 late registration)
1978	12,200 entrants (approx.)
1979	21,000 entrants (approx.)
1980-89	25,000 entrants (averaging 8,000 women)
1990-91	40,000 entrants
1992-93	45,000 entrants (averaging 15,000 women)

RESULTS

1970
Men
1. Jeff Galloway (GA) 32:21.6
2. Joel Majors (GA) 33:12
3. Michael Caldwell (SC) 35:52
4. Charles Patterson (GA) 36:21
5. David Senechalle (GA) 36:39

Women
1. Gayle Barron (GA) 49:13
2. Joan Rogers (GA) 53:29
3. Maria Birdseye (GA) 56:07

1971
Men
1. Bill Herron (FL) 30:58
2. Scott Eden (GA) 31:30
3. Lee Fidler (SC) 31:53

* Because some runners listed only a Track Club affiliation on their entry forms, all states of residence are not known.

4. Jimmy Knight (GA) 32:21
5. P.J. Leddy (TN) 32:24

Women
1. Gayle Barron (GA) 45:17
2. Maria Birdseye (GA) 57:11
3. Diane Marks (U.S.) 64:30

1972
Men
1. Scott Eden (GA) 31:10
2. Kenneth Layne (U.S.) 32:07
3. Coleman Spalding (U.S.) 32:11
4. David Bishop (GA) 32:54
5. Steve Bolt (AL) 33:07

Women
1. Gillian Valk (GA) 47:42
2. Julia Emmons (GA) 52:58
3. Linda McFarland (U.S.) 54:32
4. Marie Birdseye (GA) 55:19
5. Louise MacTyre (GA) 58:06

1973
Men
1. Bill Blewett (TX) 31:22
2. Scott Eden (GA) 31:26
3. Jon Slaughter (U.S.) 31:53
4. Don Kennedy (U.S.) 32:05
5. Dennis Spencer (U.S.) 32:26

Women
1. Gayle Barron (GA) 40:37
2. Gillian Valk (GA) 47:55
3. Becky Sears (GA) 52:00
4. Julia Emmons (GA) 52:04
5. Karen Gamel (GA) 52:18

1974
Men
1. Wayne Roach (GA) 30:47
2. Lee Fidler (U.S.) 31:24
3. Donald E. Kennedy (TX) 31:28
4. Barry Brown (FL) 31:32
5. David McKannan (AL) 31:34

Women
1. Gayle Barron (GA) 38:40
2. Karen Gamel (GA) 44:20
3. Becky Sears (U.S.) 46:40
4. Lisa Sayler (U.S.) 46:46
5. Lisa Lorrain (GA) 46:52

1975
Men
1. Ed Leddy (Ire.) 29:52
2. Barry Brown (FL) 30:10
3. Scott Eden (GA) 30:20
4. Jeff Galloway (GA) 30:26
5. Bill Haviland (U.S.) 31:02

Women
1. Gayle Barron (GA) 38:04
2. Janice Gage (FL) 39:26
3. Cathy Viegler (U.S.) 40:48
4. Tracy Siegler (U.S.) 41:18
5. Carol Vaux (U.S.) 42:50

1976
Men
1. Don Kardong (WA) 29:14
2. Bill Rodgers (MA) 29:16
3. Ed Leddy (Ire.) 29:41
4. Jeff Galloway (GA) 30:23
5. Steve Bolt (AL) 30:32

Women
1. Janice Gage (FL) 39:12
2. Laura Ledbetter (U.S.)
3. Tara Myler (GA)
4. Lisa Lorrain (GA)
5. Nancy Parker (GA) 41:40
(No times because of confusion at finish chute.)

1977
Men
1. Frank Shorter (U.S.) 29:19
2. Bill Rodgers (U.S.) 29:26
3. Don Kardong (WA) 30:08
4. Robbie Perkins (U.S.) 30:11
5. Thomas Childers (U.S.) 30:16

Women
1. Peg Neppel (IA) 36:00
2. Phyllis Hines (U.S.) 36:20
3. Janice Gage (U.S.) 36:53
4. Lisa Lorrain (U.S.) 37:10
5. Gayle Barron (GA) 38:00

1978
Men
1. Mike Roche (U.S.) 28:59.3
2. Greg Myers (U.S.) 29:15.9
3. Ralph King (U.S.) 29:19.9
4. Robert Anastasio (U.S.) 29:39.6
5. Ed Leddy (Ire.) 29:44.0

Women
1. Mary Decker (U.S.) 33:52
2. Julie Shea (U.S.) 36:47.6
3. Mary Shea (U.S.) 36:58.3
4. Shirley Silsby (U.S.) 37:11.0
5. Laura Ledbetter (U.S.) 37:12.0

1979
Men
1. Craig Virgin (U.S.) 28:30.5
2. Mike Roche (U.S.) 28:54.6
3. Steve Foster (FL) 29:13.0
4. Stan Mavis (CO) 29:16.7
5. Tony Staynings (KY) 29:21.6

Women
1. Heather Carmichael (NZ) 33:39
2. Patti Lyons (MA) 34:20.46
3. Karen Petley (U.S.) 34:45.3
4. Mary Shea (U.S.) 35:27.1
5. Karen Bridges (OK) 35:28.1

1980
Men
1. Craig Virgin (IL) 28:39.04
2. George Malley (MD) 29:19.1
3. Peter Pfitzinger (NY) 29:23.99
4. Kyle Heffner (CO) 29:24.7
5. Sosthenes Bitok (Ken) 29:25.0

Women
1. Patti Lyons-Catalano (MA) 32:48.54

2. Carol Urish (TX) 34:31.1
3. Cathie Twomey (OR) 35:01.57
4. Aileen O'Connor (MD) 35:11.6
5. Gayle Olinek (CA) 35:38.8

1981
Men
1. Craig Virgin (IL) 28:04
2. Rod Dixon (NZ) 28:11
3. Adrian Leek (Wal) 28:24
4. Bruce Bickford (MA) 28:27
5. Mark Nenow (KY) 28:32

Women
1. Allison Roe (NZ) 32:39
2. Anne Audain (NZ) 33:18
3. Sue King (AL) 33:38
4. Glenys Quick (NZ) 33:43
5. Aileen O'Connor (MD) 33:46

1982
Men
1. Jon Sinclair (CO) 28:17
2. Michael Musyoki (Ken) 28:22
3. Adrian Leek (Wal) 28:29
4. Gabriel Kamau (Ken) 28:43
5. Sosthenes Bitok (Ken) 28:48

Women
1. Anne Audain (NZ) 32:36
2. Linda McLennen (FL) 34:04
3. Eleanor Simonsick (D.C.) 34:18
4. Sue King (AL) 34:42
5. Beth Sheridan (U.S.) 34:49

1983
Men
1. Michael Musyoki (Ken) 28:21.20
2. Joseph Nzau (Ken) 28:21.80
3. Kurt Pfeffer (CO) 28:48.10
4. Rudy Chape (IN) 29:03.60
5. Duncan McDonald (CA) 29:06.50

Women
1. Grete Waitz (Nor) 32:00.20
2. Dorthe Rasmussen (Den) 33:13.10
3. Linda McLennan (FL) 33:27.0

4. Sue King (AL) 33:49.80
5. Debby Eide (OR) 33.51.50

1984
Men
1. Filbert Bayi (Tan) 28:35
2. Ashley Johnson (So. Af.) 28:42
3. Adrian Leek (WAL) 28.54
4. Craig Virgin (IL) 29:02
5. Julian Goater (ENG) 29:07

Women
1. Betty Springs (NC) 32:55
2. Carol McLatchie (TX) 33:03
3. Marty Cooksey (OR) 33:16
4. Maureen Custy (CO) 33:24
5. Joan Nesbit (NC) 33:37

1985
Men
1. Michael Musyoki (Ken) 27:58
2. Joseph Nzau (Ken) 28:07
3. Simeon Kigen (Ken) 28:17
4. Jerry Kiernan (Ire) 28:28
5. John Tuttle (GA) 28:34

Women
1. Grete Waitz (Nor) 32:02
2. Judi St. Hilaire (MA) 32:32
3. Suzanne Girard (DC) 32:46
4. Ellen Reynolds (NC) 32:47
5. PattiSue Plumer (CA) 32:56

1986
Men
1. John Doherty (Ire) 27:56
2. Michael Musyoki (Ken) 28:00
3. Ed Eyestone (UT) 28:07
4. John Tuttle (GA) 28:21
5. Adrian Leek (Wal) 28:28

Women
1. Grete Waitz (Nor) 32:10
2. Marty Cooksey (MO) 32:18
3. Sue Berenda (Can) 32:49
4. Cyndie Welte (OH) 32:58
5. Margaret Thomas (GA) 33:06

1987
Men
1. Joseph Nzau (Ken) 28:34
2. Gidamis Shahanga (Tan) 28:38
3. Bruce Bickford (U.S.) 28:43
4. Peter Koech (Ken) 28:47
5. Rob de Castella (Aus) 28:47

Women
1. Lynn Jennings (NH) 32:22
2. Teresa Ornduff (VA) 32:39
3. Marty Cooksey (MO) 33:04
4. Sue Berenda (Can) 33:11
5. Ria Van Landeghem (Bel) 33:15

1988
Men
1. J.P. Ndayisenga (Bel) 28:17
2. Mark Curp (MO) 28:20
3. John Tuttle (GA) 28:31
4. Sam Ngatia (Ken) 28:38
5. Mark Conover (CA) 28:39

Women
1. Grete Waitz (Nor) 32:10
2. Ria Van Landeghem (Bel) 32:38
3. Christine McMiken (NZ) 32:53
4. Teresa Ornduff (VA) 33:06
5. Barbara Moore (NZ) 33:21

1989
Men
1. Ibrahim Hussein (Ken) 28:13
2. Mark Nenow (CA) 28:14
3. William Musyoki (Ken) 28:34
4. Alejandro Cruz (Mex) 28:38
5. Juose Luis Cheula (Mex) 28:44

Women
1. Judi St. Hilaire (MA) 32:05
2. Cathy O'Brien (NH) 32:06
3. Barbara Moore (NZ) 32:37
4. Tina Ljunberg (Swe) 32:54
5. Monica Joyce (Ire) 32:56

1990

Men
1. Dionicio Ceron (Mex) 28:23
2. Marcos Barreto (Mex) 28:27
3. Jaquin Pinheiro (Port) 28:30
4. Steve Spence (CO) 28:32
5. Stanley Mandebele (TX) 28:33

Women
1. Cathy O'Brien (NH) 32:04
2. Carla Buerskena (Neth) 32:22
3. Maria Trujillo (AZ) 32:26
4. Patty Murray (CO) 32:39
5. Helen Moros (NZ) 32:47

1991

Men
1. Ed Eyestone (UT) 28:34
2. Alejandro Cruz (Mex) 28:39
3. Steve Kogo (CO) 28:39
4. Mark Plaatjes (CO) 28:43
5. Jon Sinclair (CO) 28:47

Women
1. Dorthe Rasmussen (Den) 32:42
2. Katerina Khramenkova (Belarus) 32:45
3. Kristy Johnson (OR) 33:04
4. Kim Jones (WA) 33:23
5. Maria Trujillo (CA) 33:39

1992

Men
1. Sammy Lelei (Ken) 27:57
2. Godfrey Kiprotich (Ken) 28:13
3. Benson Masya (Ken) 28:25
4. Keith Brantly (FL) 28:36
5. John Treacy (Ire) 28:39

Women
1. Francie Larrieu Smith (TX) 31:49
2. Cathy O'Brien (NH) 32:05
3. Albina Galliamova (CIS) 32:46
4. Helen Moros (NZ) 32:51
5. Wanda Panfil (Pol) 32:57

1993

Men
1. Thomas Osano (Ken) 28:05
2. Sammy Lelei (Ken) 28:10
3. Kimkemboi Kimeli (Ken) 28:21
4. Lucketz Swartboi (Nam) 28:24
5. Alejandro Cruz (Mex) 28:27

Women
1. Uta Pippig (Ger) 32:15
2. Anne Marie Letko (NJ) 32:20
3. Colleen De Reuck (So. Af.) 32:58
4. Nadia Prasad (France) 33:03
5. Valentina Yegorova (Rus) 33:06

WHEELCHAIR RACE

Year	Name	Time
Women		
1983	Candace Cable	31:34
1984	Sharon Hedrick	29:17
1985	Candace Cable-Brooks	30:22
1986	Candace Cable-Brooks	30:21
1987	Candace Cable-Brooks	30:38
1988	Candace Cable-Brooks	27:54
1989	Sharon Hedrick	26:48
1990	Ann Cody-Morris	25:29
1991	Jean Driscoll	23:46
1992	Connie Hansen	24:01
1993	Louise Sauvage	24:12

*No women's division race in 1982

Year	Name	Time
Men		
1982	George Murray	27:38
1983	George Murray	26:50
1984	George Murray	26:45
1985	George Murray	25:24
1986	Jim Martinson	24:22
1987	Craig Blanchette	25:08
1988	Mustapha Badid	23:00
1989	Craig Blanchette	21:52
1990	Doug Kennedy	21:09
1991	Craig Blanchette	20:17
1992	Craig Blanchette	20:07
1993	Paul Wiggins	19:58

ALL-TIME TOP 50 PERFORMANCES

Men
1. John Doherty (Ire) 27:56 (1986)
2. Sammy Lelei (Ken) 27:57 (1992)
3. Michael Musyoki (Ken) 27:58 (1985)
4. Michael Musyoki (Ken) 28:00 (1986)
5. Craig Virgin (IL) 28:04 (1981)
6. Thomas Osano (Ken) 28:05 (1993)
7. Joseph Nzau (Ken) 28:07 (1985)
   Ed Eyestone (UT) 28:07 (1986)
9. Sammy Lelei (Ken) 28:10 (1993)
10. Rod Dixon (NZ) 28:11 (1981)
11. Ibrahim Hussein (Ken) 28:13 (1989)
    Godgrey Kiprotich (Ken) 28:13 (1992)
13. Mark Nenow (CA) 28:14 (1989)
14. Jon Sinclair (CO) 28:17 (1982)
    Simeon Kigen (Ken) 28:17 (1985)
    J.P. Ndayisenga (Bel) 28:17 (1988)
17. Mark Curp (MO) 28:20 (1988)
18. John Tuttle (GA) 28:21 (1986)
    Kimkemboi Kimeli (Ken) 28:21 (1993)
20. Michael Musyoki (Ken) 28:22 (1982)
    Michael Musyoki (Ken) 28:22 (1983)
    Joseph Nzau (Ken) 28:22 (1983)
23. Dionicio Ceron (Mex) 28:23 (1990)
24. Adrian Leek (Wal) 28:24 (1981)
    Lucketz Swartboi (Nam) 28:24 (1993)
26. Benson Masya (Ken) 28:25 (1992)
27. Bruce Bickford (MA) 28:27 (1981)
    Ibrahim Hussein (Ken) 28:27 (1985)
    Marcos Barreto (Mex) 28:27 (1990)
    Alejandro Cruz (Mex) 28:27 (1993)
31. Jerry Kiernan (Ire) 28:28 (1985)
    Adrian Leek (Wal) 28:28 (1986)
33. Guillermo Serrano (Mex) 28:29 (1986)
    Adrian Leek (Wal) 28:29 (1982)
35. Ronald Lanzoni (CR) 28:30 (1986)
    Jaquin Pinheiro (Port) 28:30 (1990)
37. Craig Virgin (IL) 28:31 (1979)
    John Tuttle (GA) 28:31 (1988)
39. Mark Nenow (KY) 28:32 (1981)
    Steve Spence (CO) 28:32 (1990)
41. Stanley Mandebele (TX) 28:33 (1990)
42. John Tuttle (GA) 28:34 (1985)
    Gidamis Shahanga (Tan) 28:34 (1986)
    Joseph Nzau (Ken) 28:34 (1987)
    William Musyoki (Ken) 28:34 (1989)
    Ed Eyestone (UT) 28:34 (1991)
47. Filbert Bayi (Tan) 28:35 (1984)
    Ed Eyestone (UT) 28:35 (1990)
49. Benji Durden (GA) 28:36 (1981)
    Adrian Leek (Wal) 28:36 (1985)
    Keith Brantly (FL) 28:36 (1992)
    Gideon Mutisya (Ken) 28:36 (1993)

Women
1. Francie Larrieu Smith (TX) 31:49 (1992)
2. Grete Waitz (Nor) 32:01 (1993)
3. Grete Waitz (Nor) 32:02 (1985)
4. Cathy O'Brien (NH) 32:04 (1990)
5. Judi St. Hilaire (MA) 32:05 (1989)
   Cathy O'Brien (NH) 32:05 (1992)
7. Cathy O'Brien (NH) 32:06 (1989)
8. Grete Waitz (Nor) 32:10 (1986)
   Grete Waitz (Nor) 32:10 (1988)
10. Uta Pippig (Ger) 32:15 (1993)
11. Marty Cooksey (MO) 32:18 (1986)
12. Anne Marie Letko (NJ) 32:20 (1993)
13. Lynn Jennings (NH) 32:22 (1987)
    Carla Buerskins (Neth) 32:22 (1990)
15. Maria Trujillo (AZ) 32:26 (1990)
16. Judi St. Hilaire (MA) 32:32 (1985)
17. Anne Audain (NZ) 32:36 (1982)
18. Barbara Moore (NZ) 32:37 (1989
19. Ria Van Landeghem (Bel) 32:38 (1988)
20. Allison Roe (NZ) 32:39 (1981)
    Teresa Ornduff (VA) 32:39 (1987)
    Patty Murray (CO) 32:39 (1990)
23. Dorthe Rasmussen (Den) 32:42 (1991)
24. Katarina Khramenkova (Belarus) 32:45 (1991)
25. Suzanne Girard (DC) 32:46 (1985)
    Albina Galliamova (CIS) 32:46 (1992)
27. Ellen Reynolds (NC) 32:47 (1985)
    Helen Moros (NZ) 32:47 (1990)
29. Patti Lyons-Catalono (MA) 32:49 (1980)
    Sue Berenda (Can) 32:49 (1986)
31. Helen Moros (NZ) 32:51
32. Christine McMiken (NZ) 32:53 (1988)

You may think your chowhound is a bottomless pit, but his stomach does have a maximum capacity. This varies a great deal among breeds—from one quart in a toy breed to two gallons in a large breed.

ACKNOWLEDGMENTS:

I would like to thank the
following people for their
encouragement: Forrest
Rogers, who would have
been my training partner if
we had done any training
(we've never finished last);
Jack Wilkinson, who appreci-
ates a good play on words;
Sharon Robb, who during
the Lillehammer Olympics
would ask me, "Karen, have
you finished your book?";
Frank Zang, who was too
polite to ask about the book,
but wondered, and Rheta
Grimsley Johnson, who gave
me my first writing job.
    And special thanks to the
Atlanta Track Club and the
Atlanta Journal-Constitution
photography department,
without whom this book
would not be possible.

–*Karen Rosen*

*Susie Langle, 95 years old,
cheers runners in 1988.*